DEADLY PROFESSORS

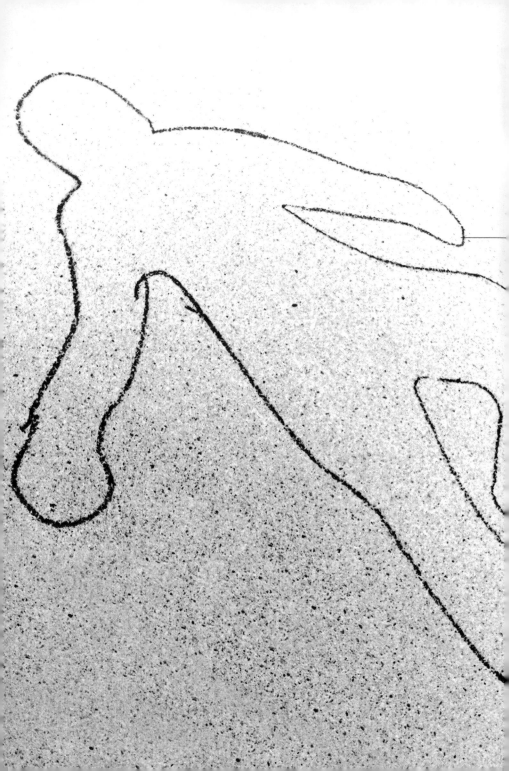

DEADLY PROFESSORS

A Faculty Development Mystery

Thomas B. Jones

STERLING, VIRGINIA

Sty/us

Published by Stylus Publishing, LLC
22883 Quicksilver Drive
Sterling, Virginia 20166–2102

Library of Congress Cataloging-in-Publication-Data
Jones, Thomas B., 1942–
    Deadly professors : workshop discussion questions
and other faculty development activities / Thomas B.
Jones.—1st ed.
        p.   cm.
    Includes bibliographical references and index.
    ISBN 978–1-57922–449–3 (cloth : alk. paper)
    ISBN 978–1-57922–450–9 (pbk. : alk. paper)
        1. College personnel management.   2. Teacher-
administrator relationships.   3. Teachers' workshops.
I. Title.
LB2331.66.J64   2010
378.1'1—dc22   2009050711

13-digit ISBN: 978–1-57922–449–3 (cloth)
13-digit ISBN: 978–1-57922–450–9 (paper)

Printed in the United States of America

All first editions printed on acid free paper
that meets the American National Standards Institute
Z39–48 Standard.

Bulk Purchases

Quantity discounts are available for use in
workshops and for staff development. Call
1–800–232–0223

First Edition, 2010

10   9   8   7   6   5   4   3   2   1

To Susan, Buirge and Katie, Jessica and Alex, Christie, Tony, Don, and all the Joneses, Houses, Halls, and Schaacks—here and beyond.

This is a work of fiction, of course, and most of the names and characters in this novel are imagined, invented, or the result of a retired professor's addled brain.

Välkommen University Arms and Motto

Audio Video Disco Animadverto Do

A Note on Tyr

Tyr, one of the gods of Norse mythology, represents courage and hero-ism and is depicted as having only a left hand, his right having been severed by the monstrous and mythic wolf Fenrir. He is always por-trayed holding a sword, which is also considered a symbol of justice. His name in Old English, Tīw, gave rise to today's Tuesday (Tīw's Day).

AUTHOR'S NOTE AND ACKNOWLEDGMENTS

Like its forerunner, *The Missing Professor* (Sterling, VA: Stylus, 2005), this book combines discussion stories and informal case studies with what a friend labeled a "cheesy, but occasionally funny" academic mystery. Oh well. But allow me to argue, with due moderation, that my fusion of discussion stories/informal case studies with an academic mystery works well as a jumping-off point for faculty development workshops, teaching circles, new faculty orientation, and brown-bag conversations among professors, administrators, and academic staff.

More often than not, the best faculty development takes place as a result of simple, easygoing opportunities for people to gather and discuss teaching and learning, academic issues, and professional lives. Despite what much of the public thinks, the workdays of professors are jam-packed with a crush of activities. Idle hours are few and far between. For busy faculty to secure a few moments on campus to think and talk about what they do—and how to do it better—is a difficult task. I hope the informal approach of this book and the variety of ways it can be used for faculty development promotes vigorous discussions without an excessive amount of meeting time spent on planning and organizing.

Deadly Professors features a variety of issues and dilemmas concerning faculty roles and responsibilities; senior faculty and retirement; new students; adjunct faculty; multiculturalism; teaching and technology; professorial blogging, twittering, and whatever; the first day of class; curriculum requirements; intercollegiate athletics; classroom indoctrination; and academic freedom. These issues and dilemmas are intended to provoke discussion, and at times the book's characters take positions and make judgments that might rub some readers the wrong way. Even the main character, Professor Jack Ramble, is not without his flaws, and intentionally so. Despite serving as an administrator at times during my own career, I confess to having a bit too much fun picking on those who guide the rest of us in higher education. My foibles aside, workshop discussions based on this book should be lively and, I hope, always balanced with respect and goodwill among those who participate (sort of like a faculty meeting—right?).

My guess is that faculty and others will have little difficulty identifying issues and questions for discussion, finding supplementary readings and resources, and applying expertise and skills to their best advantage. To help things along, if necessary, I have listed some general discussion questions and useful materials at the conclusion of the book.

My years in academe have brought me into contact with many wonderful colleagues and students. I thank one and all for their friendship and for what they have taught me. Among those who deserve special mention in regard to this project are Susan Keiko Nathan, Donna Blacker, Rich and Prudy Hall, Carl Petsch, and Ed Nuhfer. Ed's wonderful summer gathering in Leadville, Colorado (Boot Camp for Professors) gave me an opportunity to try out several chapters with small groups of well-informed and expert college teachers. I owe all concerned a great debt of gratitude for their time, insights, and constructive comments.

CHAPTER 1

Sunday Evening

Damn the little wretches. Another empty beer can littered Professor Roland Norris's driveway. The outraged academic glared at the offending object, punching at the steering wheel of his automobile.

Almost every night, the dorm rats drank themselves silly at the Golden Gopher Pub, then staggered back to the Välkommen University campus with six-packs of Grain Belt beer in hand. Norris could hear the hell-raising at all hours as drunken fools stumbled through the walkways of a small landscape architecture park near his townhouse. He'd complained to the vice president for Physical Plant Services, Kevin Greene, but all the protest gained was a hideous hedge of some bristly sort, planted as a barrier along Norris's driveway. The shrubbery did nothing to dissuade the students from lobbing over their empties.

Norris struggled to control his growing outrage. He'd been so jazzed by his debut appearance on Channel 3's *Twin Cities Rumpus Room* earlier that evening, it seemed a shame to lose the warm glow he felt. He took a deep, cleansing breath and closed his eyes, recalling special moments of the TV broadcast. He'd done his best to ooze civility and come across as a stand-up guy, although sustaining such alien personal behavior throughout the two-hour broadcast was no easy task. Launching well-rehearsed bursts of moral outrage and assaulting others' claims to intelligence suited him best. Perhaps his ex-wife, that god-awful shrew, had been right for once when she warned him about his penchant for a certain pit bull swagger. Norris would have liked to sink his teeth into the panel of guest experts but had suppressed the impulse, sticking to his game plan. As the final credits rolled, the wily professor made his play for a permanent slot on *Rumpus Room*, betting he could make the public ethicist thing into a real moneymaker. To his surprise, the program host and producers all complained of pressing business and left the studio. In their wake, Norris stood on the empty set with a pimply-faced, gum-chewing student intern who persisted in asking dumb questions about a career in college teaching.

Driving home to St. Paul from Minneapolis, close to midnight, Norris mused on what great fun it was to be so witty . . . so smart . . . so well educated. At one of the many stoplights on University Avenue, he checked his reflection in the rearview mirror, practicing a knowing smile for future publicity photos. After a loud honk from the car behind him, Norris took a right turn on Snelling Avenue in the direction of Välkommen University where he was an associate professor of philosophy and religious studies.

Passing by a string of dreary stores and inelegant apartment buildings near campus, Norris thought about the university's past—in particular, Välkommen U's founder, Inga Skoog Gadda, heiress to the Gadda Swedish Frozen Foods colossus.

In the early 1980s, Inga had made available millions of dollars from her family's business empire to establish the university. According to a story Norris heard upon joining the faculty, Inga's father, Hjalmer Gadda, jumped into the frozen packaged foods boom of the early 1950s with a number of imaginative products—many of which had a multicultural appeal. Although Norris held no fond regard for multiculturalism—no matter what the flavor—he did appreciate profit seeking and marketing genius. Twin Cities' supermarkets now stocked Gadda frozen smoked salmon pizza, Swedish meatball tacos, rutabaga-potato dumpling Asian stir-fry, and for the less-adventuresome grocery-shopping Minnesotans, a savory walleye meatloaf. Once assuming control of Gadda foods after her father's unexpected death, Inga kept the corporate kitchens busy with her ideas. Her creativity and business acumen helped produce a welcome supplemental cash flow for Välkommen University. Vodka-infused, torsk-stuffed frozen sushi rolls? You betcha. And who among the comfort-food lovers of Viking ancestry could forgo heat-and-serve bagel bites stuffed with lutefisk?

Norris always thought Inga a most attractive, intriguing woman. In her youth, as a student at a small college in southern Minnesota, Inga's undergraduate experience included a sizzling affair with a professor of Nordic studies, Dr. Ernst Torkelson. Of course, as Norris and any true son of the North Star state could have predicted, the illicit romance came to an early and unhappy end. Professor Torkelson's jealous wife destroyed his book manuscript, *Ole and Lena Conflicted: Race, Gender, Colonialism, Urgent Sexuality, and Becoming in Trans-Nordic Jocosity*. Norris heartily approved of the manuscript scuttling, and he found justice in the fact that Inga's "love professor"—distraught over the loss of his life's scholarship—impaled himself in spectacular fashion on the prow of a reconstructed Viking ship, the centerpiece at a well-attended Twin Cities' Svenskarnas Dag festival.

While the tragedy of Inga's love affair failed to excite Norris's sympathy, he could somewhat appreciate the woman's passion for things Nordic. That passion led Inga to collect a treasure trove of rare books and letters, ice sculpture designs, genealogical records, and late twentieth-century Scandinavian pop music. As the hapless maiden converted her family estate and neighboring properties in the prestigious Summit and Snelling Avenue neighborhood into Välkommen University, she built the Skoog Museum to house her acquisitions. She also provided funding for the Torkelson School of Nordic Studies, an academic program Norris and his cronies dearly loved to slander at every opportunity, albeit in private whisperings.

Still, Norris had to admit, Inga Gadda's intense desire to build Välkommen U into a showplace of higher education offered great opportunities. A few years back, during a brief plunge in prices for prestige properties in the Summit and Snelling area, George Dingkudgel, a handsome twenty-eight-year-old real estate wunderkind, helped Inga acquire several estates adjacent to the original campus. The plan was to construct a faculty housing complex. Norris had his doubts about that scheme, especially when Inga designated Dingkudgel as the man to see the project to completion. Norris thought the path pursued by the young entrepreneur betrayed a certain lack of understanding about Inga's dreams, if not her ethnic heritage. Also, Dingkudgel employed the same architectural group responsible for the retro villages so popular in Florida. The architects added a twist, modeling their design for Välkommen U faculty housing on the country villages of the British Cotswolds region, replete with high-tech cottages dripping in ivy, a manor house replica for the university president, a public square, and a village pub. As one of Norris's friends on the faculty quipped, "This is great. All we need is a village idiot."

"Wait until fall semester starts," Norris replied. "We'll have our pick."

Never one to look a gift horse in the mouth, Norris now resided in the Bourbon-on-the-Water neighborhood (an unfortunate paraphrase by a student intern assigned to signage). His replica home, with a limestone facade and a sloping, pseudo-thatch roof, sat on the far edge of campus but within walking distance of the philosophy and religious study department's offices. As a member of the building committee, Norris lent his strong support to help secure a lucrative contract for Universal Imperative Construction, a company owned by a favorite student of the professor's from years past. Another former student, now an assistant to St. Paul's mayor, sat on Välkommen U's Board of Regents, so Norris ended up with a sweetheart deal on the only two-story unit in the complex, not to mention deep discounts on top-of-the-line carpeting, lighting, built-in appliances, an HDTV projection system, and a jumbo-size Jacuzzi. Instructing others to make moral choices wasn't a bad gig at all.

Norris stooped to pick up the beer can glowing in the light cast on the driveway from his automobile's headlamps. At that instant, powerful fingers gripped his neck from behind, yanking him backward and through the evergreen hedge. Norris yelped as his attacker flung him down on the hard ground.

Flat on his back, his neck and shoulders searing with pain, a knee pressing down on his chest, Norris's eyes watered with fear and torment.

A huge rock gripped in black-gloved fingers hovered above his face. The rock had a single word inscribed on its surface, but alas, Norris knew he had no time left for metaphysical signification.

Pete Petersen stumbled through the arboretum at dawn's light, trying his best to follow the wood chips marking his path. His feet felt light and airy, moving in directions quite opposite to his wishes.

Petersen had spent most of the night at a friend's apartment boozing and playing poker with other workers from the campus grounds crew. By 1:00 a.m. they'd run out of beer, but shots of peppermint schnapps and lime vodka kept flowing. Petersen passed out on the carpet for a couple of hours, waking with a horrendous mix of flavors curling on his tongue.

Still a bit drunk—a lot drunk—Petersen wove sideways off the path and crashed into a thicket of trees. One arm draped around a Japanese maple, holding on for dear life, he extended his foot to step over what looked like a huge log.

He screamed.

An awful keening from the arboretum jolted campus cop Terry Tredstedt from a deep sleep. As always, he'd parked his patrol car in the cul-de-sac near the arboretum hoping to catch a short nap before his shift ended. He tumbled out of the car, half kneeling beside it, allowing a few seconds for the cobwebs to clear.

The screaming came in short bursts now.

No time left to be afraid, Tredstedt told himself. Suck it up and go.

He ran through the iron gate marking the arboretum's entrance, one hand clamped on the butt of his holstered revolver and the other holding a heavy-duty flashlight, its beam tracing erratic loops across the trees ahead. He slipped on a wet patch of leaves and grass, sprawling forward on hands and knees, flashlight thumping to the earth. Tredstedt followed the beam of light extending across the ground.

He screamed.

St. Paul homicide detectives LeRon Jarvis and Robert Phan stared at the body. The victim lay face up. *It's a good thing the poor bastard was on his back*, thought Jarvis, because he didn't have much of a face left. The assailant had replaced it with a stone about the size of an Idaho potato driven with great force into the victim's forehead. Jarvis ordered one of the emergency medical techs to pry the thing from the guy's cranium. The med tech had to borrow a screwdriver for the task. The young student who had found the body whimpered, and the campus cop hugged him close as the med tech performed the extraction.

Jarvis knelt down to examine the hefty piece of granite. It had rounded corners and a smooth surface, reminding Jarvis of something he'd seen in one of those mail-order garden catalogs, engraved with a dopey inscription like, "Believe." He turned the stone over to see the other side. Despite flecks of the victim's blood and what looked like part of an eyebrow, letters etched in an artistic, painstaking script formed the killer's message: H i p p o c r i t e.

"Great. A perp who can't spell," said Jarvis.

"So you think it's a student?" Phan deposited the rock in a plastic evidence bag with a heavy sigh. The two homicide detectives had seen more than their share of murders in St. Paul over the past five years.

Jarvis bent under the yellow crime scene tape. "Hell of a way to start fall semester."

"Yeah." Phan eyeballed the murder weapon. "A philosopher's stone?"

"More like a stone wall," Jarvis muttered. "Let's rock on, Phan."

CHAPTER 2

Across campus on the day before classes started, faculty members jabbered about the murder and its traumatic effects. The consensus favored delaying the fall semester for at least a week. Jack Ramble, professor of literature and chair of his department, would have preferred not to teach for a while too, but not for the same reasons as his colleagues. His thirtieth year in academe and the thought of marching into a lecture hall full of new students gave him a strange feeling. It wasn't a case of first class jitters. Things were a bit more serious than that. Somewhere along the road from last June's graduation to the start of a new semester, he'd lost much of his excitement about teaching.

The warning signs of his academic blue funk had been abundant throughout the summer months. During June and July he'd devoted inordinate attention to time-consuming, tedious household projects. Cleaning out the garage, painting the basement walls, steaming carpets, replacing the garage doors, washing windows, edging the lawn, and a host of similar domestic ventures occupied him from dawn to dusk. Funny. He'd always hated that stuff.

In the evenings, mystery novels and mindless television viewing completed his day's activities. He even watched the local news at 10:00

7

p.m., wasting what seemed a lifetime counting how many facial expressions the news anchors could muster emoting their way through shootings, stabbings, carjackings, domestic disputes, fires, and whatever other mania the crews could dredge up from the Twin Cities and beyond. He developed a morbid fascination for the antics of the female news anchor twit. She would gaze into the camera, nodding and pursing her polished lips, cuing the viewing audience to pay heed to the oleaginous delivery of her coanchor, a master of the gelled forelock and knowing smirk. Ramble stopped watching after imagining the coanchors launching adult movie careers atop the news desk.

In the month's runup to the fall semester's first day of classes, Ramble abandoned any remaining home repairs for daily rounds of golf and hours on the practice range. Knocking six points off his handicap seemed the thing to do. He followed his golfing with a muscle-ripping workout at the university's weight room and a two-mile run. By the time he made it home, he was too tired for much of anything else but to heat a frozen dinner and maybe start another mystery novel. Physically he felt great—in as good shape as he could be at fifty-five years old. His mental side wasn't so well conditioned.

In the two and a half months since June graduation, Ramble had not spent a single moment working on his research and writing. Unlike so many summers before, he did little to prepare for his fall semester's classes. He didn't revise any of his syllabi—even the smallest fraction.

In his many years as a professor, Ramble couldn't remember ever recycling the same course materials. It didn't seem right to stand pat when a good course could always be made better by reading the latest research and fine-tuning assignments. The dulled edge of Ramble's motivation reminded him somewhat of the long months he'd spent digging out from his wife's death five years before. Nothing so serious now, of course, he assured himself. He'd get over it. A passing phase, that's all.

"You look positively disconnected." Angela Evangelista leaned against the door frame, a smile of concern on her lips. She wore a black skirt, black turtleneck sweater, and as she came to perch on the side of Ramble's desk, he couldn't help but notice her black-tinted nylons. Well before this particular moment, Ramble had determined black to be the most seductive color a woman could wear. According to his personal history of women in black, Angela Evangelista set new standards.

Ramble served on the hiring committee for the position Angela now held as director of the teaching center. She had far outclassed the other candidates, and the committee's decision to hire had been unanimous. Angela jumped into the job over the summer with a burst of high energy and good ideas. In the past, Ramble had resisted attending the faculty development workshops for professors. He didn't suspect that Angela would allow that behavior to persist. Ramble thought it might well be time to turn over a new leaf.

"Are you feeling OK?"

"I'm fine."

"Come on. What's the problem?" Angela sat on the sofa. Ramble had brought it and a side table from home when he first moved into the large corner office. There didn't seem to be much need for all that furniture at home with only him and the dog living there.

"I'm not sure. Maybe I'm burned out," Ramble said.

Angela curled her legs up, settling back into the sofa cushions. "Good. You'll make a perfect candidate for this year's workshop focus."

"What's that?"

"It's one intended for our senior faculty." Angela paused, locking her dark eyes on Ramble. He knew Angela had him grouped with the over-fifty crowd of professors. He didn't particularly like being part of that academic gang.

"I'm thinking of something like a senior faculty learning community," Angela said. "I can't seem to work out a title for the project yet. Invigorating Senior Faculty? Rejuvenating? Freshening? I don't know. You're Mr. Literature . . . help me out here."

"A number of suggestions come to mind, Angela." Ramble tried to keep a straight face. "However, I am constrained not to offer any as they may violate a recent missive from human resources."

"You are referring to the one directed at sexist pigs like yourself?"

"That's the one."

"Well, then, it's good to see you've taken your learning to heart."

Neither of them said anything for a while. Angela smiled. "What if I gave you permission to air one of your suggestions?"

"I'd rather wait until I have one that's appropriate and helpful." Ramble pretended to look through a stack of papers on his desk.

Angela wandered over to the windows overlooking the quadrangle. "So tell me why you're so burned out. Give me some specifics."

"I don't know. I guess I feel stuck—or something like that."

"Stuck?"

"Yeah. Stuck. I had all these plans for research and writing. Time seems to have slipped away."

"Come on, Ramble. You have more publications than anyone else in the whole humanities division." Angela ran her fingers across a row of journals and books he kept on a stand near the windows. She plucked a slender volume from the collection and flipped though the first few pages. "Hmmm. *Hamlin Garland: Rural Environments and American Cultural Imaginings* by Jack Ramble." She wiggled the book at him. "You've always been active as a scholar. It's not like you haven't combined teaching and publishing over all these years."

"I guess."

Ramble couldn't claim he worried about keeping up with younger colleagues in the department. He didn't see the newest faculty members as rivals, and he didn't envy their energetic quest for research grants and publications. He could hold his own and offered his help and advice when the opportunity arose. But still, he'd had bigger dreams when he finished grad school. It felt like he'd let down his former professors, not to mention himself.

"Do you have any beefs with the university?"

"Why do you ask that?"

"It's one of the things senior faculty often complain about. They feel as though they're regarded as deadwood and passed over for new initiatives."

Ramble thought about what Angela had suggested but didn't think of himself that way. "Actually, I'm not anxious to add things, and I can't say I'm dissatisfied with my opportunities here."

"If someone else felt the way you do now, what would you say?"

Ramble knew he'd been caught out by Angela's question. "I'd probably say, suck it up and quit feeling sorry for yourself."

Angela didn't reply but gave Ramble an I-gotcha look. Ramble liked the way she could hustle him into a corner. After Margaret's death, it had taken a long time to feel anything very complicated about another woman.

"Why don't we focus on your role as a teacher," Angela said.

As he watched Angela cross one elegant leg over the other, Ramble wished it was some distant age when men might simply blurt out the obvious: "Damn, Angela, you are something." He knew why he shouldn't say it, but that didn't change what he felt no matter what the faculty handbook chapter on sexual harassment warned.

"Do you think you've lost popularity with students?" Angela asked.

"I feel like I have."

Ramble remembered how it used to be. Students fought for places in his courses, and they'd line up after class to ask questions. He'd felt tuned in to his students. Several times he won teaching awards, and his Introduction to Literature had long been one of the must-take classes at the university. In the past few years, though, Ramble noticed a slow but significant change in the undergraduates that left him unsettled about his classroom skills. They didn't respond in the same way as in the past. His best jokes and humorous asides met with but a few smiles and polite laughter.

Ramble knew he'd lost touch with students' tastes in music and their reference points in popular culture. Connections he'd used so effectively in years past seemed broken. He and his students didn't talk the same language, not to mention the huge gap between their computer and communications technology know-how and his rudimentary skills. Ramble didn't own a cell phone much less understand how to use all the new technological bells and whistles for the classroom. He'd take a pass on that stuff anyway. Did students really like their professors mucking around with PowerPoint presentations, podcasts, Facebook, and all that? Did they learn better as a result?

At the least, Ramble finally had an answer to a question asked at the start of his career. A senior member of his department had organized grad students into an informal discussion group about college teaching, and they'd visited one of Ramble's classes. Ramble treated them to his 1950s "America and Literature" lecture, replete with a slide presentation, representative musical and fashion trends, dramatic readings from *Peyton Place*, commentary on dating practices, and a rip-roaring closer—his costumed, lip-synch rendition of Mark Dinning's "Teen Angel." At lunch with the visitors after class, their professor asked, "How will you teach when you're an old man like me?" Ramble could only think of himself now as a pale shadow of his former teaching self. His slideshows and impressions were out of date, and his musical horizons increasingly limited to the oldies stations. Worst of all, the issues and controversies he'd cared about so passionately left his students listless, and "spaced out." *Even my slang is old hat,* Ramble lamented. *Old hat?* Talk about being out of it.

The things that ignited Ramble's protest and idealistic spirit in his youth were so much ancient history to students. It didn't seem as if his teaching had done much to make the world a better place. He doubted the vast majority of students passing through his classroom emerged as changed beings with their intellectual, political, aesthetic, and personal horizons greatly expanded. Ramble was a long way now from the romantic view he'd entertained about being a college professor at the start of his career. He remembered telling a friend he wanted to be a professor so he could make a difference. His father, a college history professor, listened patiently one late night to Ramble's undergraduate hopes for humankind, the nation, and his future career. "You might want to review your world history notes," the old man said, passing his empty scotch glass across the table for a refill. Decades after that night, even if he didn't like doing so, Ramble fully appreciated the wisdom of his father's simple suggestion.

When he explained it all to Angela, she listened but didn't seem to be that sympathetic. A woman in her mid-forties, she probably regarded Ramble much the same way his students did.

"So to sum it up," Ramble said, "I'm facing my declining years of teaching without much confidence, little idealism, and a bag full of useless humor, metaphors, and stories."

Angela gave him a sympathetic smile. She gathered up her briefcase and purse, preparing to leave.

"So you're going to leave me in this predicament?"

Angela rested her hand on the doorknob. She gave him a look Ramble interpreted as, "Poor baby."

"Maybe you should put on your department chair's hat and think of what you might do with a faculty member who's tired of teaching and down in the dumps like you."

Ramble did know a few senior faculty who also seemed to have lost their motivation for teaching. Asking some key questions and putting together a package of focused sessions on teaching might be just the thing to revitalize the old dogs. It was worth a try. Ramble couldn't believe that his colleagues in the department felt good about losing their edge. Plus, they had experiences and skills to share with those new to the game.

"Why don't you come to this workshop? Your problem may be in the way you're thinking about teaching." Angela searched in her briefcase and came out with a broadside titled, "It's About Student Learning, Stupid! Rethinking the Paradigm." She made a sour face at Ramble. "I told you I'm no good at workshop titles."

"Indeed."

Angela shouldered her briefcase and opened the office door to leave.

"Keep That Spark Alive?" Ramble turned to his computer, pretending to study the list of e-mails on the screen. "Stay in the Game?"

"What?"

"Just suggestions for your new workshop title."

Angela frowned. "I don't know."

Ramble turned to his computer screen, clicked open an e-mail, hiding a smile. The message held a link to the online student newspaper update. A headline read: "Professor Norris Had On-Campus Enemies."

No kidding.

Ramble pushed the delete key.

Five minutes passed before Angela stood again in Ramble's office doorway. The expression on her face revealed she'd thought about his suggestions for a workshop title.

"Baaad dog!"

Ramble counted himself lucky she didn't have a rolled-up newspaper.

CHAPTER 3

"The police department has promised to leave no stone unturned."

Newly appointed Välkommen University president George Dingkudgel had for the moment forgotten the circumstances of Roland Norris's violent rendezvous with the Grim Reaper. "We will hope most fervently that whosoever has slain our precious colleague will meet with everlasting damnation."

President Dingkudgel had assembled the troops for the morning in-service session to kick off the new semester, but given the murder of Professor Norris the night before, special words of remembrance and encouragement about campus life after "the immense tragedy that has befallen our institution" seemed imperative. As the president launched into an off-the-cuff eulogy, Ramble's blood began to curdle. In his mind, an honest benediction for the fallen professor would read something like, "Dear Professor Norris—a lying, loutish, pompous, annoying academic fathead was he."

Professors Ramble and Norris had tangled often since their arrival on the Välkommen University campus two decades earlier. But only once over the years had Ramble really lost his temper. Norris took too many potshots at the required introductory literature course during a general education meeting, and Ramble confronted him in the hallway between classes the next day. Norris called Ramble a fascist and tried to shove his way free. Ramble shoved back . . . just a little. Norris flopped to the floor like a flounder, drawing gasps from a hallway packed with student onlookers. Faking a back injury, Norris wailed at thunderstruck students to summon the campus police. To their credit, as Ramble recalled, none of the onlookers thought it necessary to do so.

Assistant dean Abel Billings called the two professors on the carpet for the incident the next day—he even asked the pair to shake hands like a couple of ten-year-olds. Ramble laughed at Billings for suggesting the peace ritual, rejecting it out of hand, so to speak. But the two feuding professors kept their clashes to the realm of words after that. Ramble was taken aback at Norris's demise. But in light of their past history, Ramble had no intention of attending a memorial service for that lard ass.

After paying due attention to the murder, President Dingkudgel jumped quickly to the real business of the meeting, although first assuring the assembled faculty that "Professor Norris would have wanted us to move forward for the betterment of the university and its students." Then, without missing a beat, the president introduced what he characterized as a "significant, cutting-edge, actionable, Management by Vision All-University Future Assurance Initiative." Ramble knew one thing for sure: faculty in his literature department wouldn't touch a vision thing with a ten-foot pole.

Dingkudgel's career path included not a wit of academic management experience as far as Ramble could tell. His appointment owed in large part to a close relationship with Inga Gadda who seemed desperate at the moment for the companionship of an adoring, chivalrous younger man. Dingkudgel, the man in question, had graduated from a small, private Bible college in northwestern South Dakota with a double major in business administration and free-market theology. Upon graduation, he hit the road to the Twin Cities with nary a backward glance. There he parlayed his educational background into local fame and fortune as a real estate sales associate. The youthful business whiz shot through the ranks of Twin Cities' realtors to the executive presidency of Paradise Investments. Yet, at the top of his game at age twenty-eight, Dingkudgel apparently suffered a brief crisis of identity, perhaps attributable to an innate spirituality. The result? He seemingly lost his deep passion for home sales.

According to one of Ramble's friends in the administration, it took a three-day retreat to the balcony of his million-dollar condominium overlooking Lake Calhoun for Dingkudgel to get back on keel. Ultimately he found his new purpose, a special life's calling. Within a week, working in what could only be called a mystical frenzy, Dingkudgel conceived, planned, and secured bottom-dollar financing for the Eternal Communal Nonsectarian Community of Gopher Valley—a tree-lined, flower-rich acreage, sprawled over some two square miles of prime real estate, smack in the center of a booming, outer-ring Twin Cities' suburb on a major state highway just beyond a humungous shopping mall anchored by a mega Walmart and a Super Target. Behind a massive spired entrance with sparkling waterfalls and a bell tower, Dingkudgel constructed 1,500 upscale housing units and a complex of substantial buildings replete with a multifunction retreat center, bingo hall, movie theater, health spa, and yoga training temple—all of which overlooked a private, white sand beach on Lake Lazy Fair. Ramble imagined that merely describing Dingkudgel's sublime architectural triumph must turn visitors breathless.

Unfortunately, and certainly not the young entrepreneur's fault, the Gopher Valley project reached a stasis, financially speaking, less than five years after its completion. The several Twin Cities' housing empires bursting through the suburbs exhausted the frontier available for expansionary annexation. Rumor had it that shortly after a quarterly financial report, the priests-of-the-bottom-line within Gopher Valley's board of directors advised Dingkudgel he might want to consider new pastures. It was then the defrocked realtor got the call from Inga Gadda to lead the academic flock at Välkommen U.

As Ramble and others noticed, the matriarch of Gadda Swedish Frozen Foods and Välkommen U feared for the future. The university had struggled lately, and its endowment refused to match the financial demands of building maintenance, administrative and faculty salaries, and plans for new graduate programs. So Inga looked close at hand for someone to turn things around. It appeared to Ramble and to most on the Välkommen U faculty that Inga trusted Dingkudgel implicitly, and that his talents were writ large on her mind and heart. He seemed the perfect leader to his patroness, and his steady visits for Sunday dinners at the Gadda mansion didn't hurt. Dingkudgel seemed just the man destined to take Inga's beloved university into a brighter future.

Ramble had to admit, Dingkudgel's ascension to a top job at the institution did have a certain symmetry. His previous line of work demanded strong talents for public speaking, fund-raising, and drawing together a large, diverse, frequently wacky congregation of faithful homebuyers.

"Cultivation of excellence, colleagues. That's what we have been called to accomplish. Unity, my friends. We must work together as a team." Dingkudgel continued his pitch, and took a hasty swig of water from the glass placed near him by a thoughtful aide.

"Awrrggh." August Pettibone, the music department's expert on classical pregrunge harmonics, laid his head in his hands, muttering to himself. "What are we supposed to cultivate? Failure? I am *not* a team player. I refuse to don any such helmet and rush to the gridiron of academic games. I don't even like the damn Vikings!"

"Be kind, August," Ramble counseled.

Truth be told, Ramble shared his colleague's distaste for Dingkudgel's business school leadership lingo, acquired during an intensive, six-week, online MBA program after which he wrote a management text (a self-published, fifty-page hardcover volume, *Management by Vision: Looking Forward to Success in the Wink of an Eye*) that earned him an honorary doctorate from his alma mater, now a part of the state community college system. Admonitions about working together and fostering collegiality made sense to many faculty, *in the abstract,* but Ramble bet nine out of ten professors would champion dissent, nonconformity, and gadflyism as a necessary, if not more comfortable, stance to preserve unfettered academic debate and academic freedom. As a department chair, Ramble all too often wondered what it would be like if faculty adopted some general code of collegiality. But really, would his group of academics routinely and easily march to the same tune?

Unlike some multinational corporate division, Ramble's literature department faculty simply did not think of themselves in terms of a team. They were a diverse collection of faculty members, talented teachers and researchers. Like most college faculty, literature department members had, as one higher education management expert described it, "multiple missions," and thus didn't have clear, everyday tasks that everyone shared. Ramble didn't have a good description at hand for how the department's members at times functioned at their collective best.

He *did* believe the faculty could build a type of teamwork and community on the basis of their academic interests and hopes for the department's students. He knew his colleagues had dreams of excellence and worked together every so often with great results. They'd also demonstrated a capacity for sincere collegiality (really, they had). But how could Ramble extend and expand the best qualities of his department for more than the transitory moment? What could he do as a department chair to promote collegiality? He assumed it was one of his responsibilities. So far he had few immediate, satisfactory answers available to his questions.

"Management by Vision requires faculty and especially department chairs to cast aside their individual autonomies and align with the larger values and goals of our university's educational mission." Dingkudgel moved from behind the portable lectern bearing the university seal and motto to walk up the center aisle of the auditorium. His practiced voice boomed across the room as if a microphone were but a stage prop. He urged the faculty to look at the big picture, to entertain others' ideas, to build strategically for the future.

"Gad. I much preferred our former leader with all his earthly faults to our current minister of the academic-business gospel." August rubbed his balding pate. Ramble noticed a few wispy hairs falling to his colleague's shirt collar. "Why do I even have to think about all this crud? We spent more than enough time two years ago putting together mission statements and all that rot. Everybody forgot them the minute the semester ended."

"I know, I know." Ramble held his voice at a whisper, hoping August would get the hint.

Dingkudgel's premapped circuit of the auditorium brought him near the row where Ramble and August sat. After a brief review of university decision making and the roles of Välkommen U's administrators and faculty in that process, he paused in the aisle, head bowed, the elegant and buffed fingertips of one hand touching his forehead.

"What is this? The agony of St. George?" Luella DeiSel, a well-respected, feminist guerrilla pastoral poet sitting on the aisle next to Ramble shook her head at the academic president's dramatic pose.

"I must remind you." Dingkudgel turned his gaze to the auditorium's skylight. "Demanding full participation on all decisions is a temptation faculty might well avoid unless you are ready to take the responsibility for implementation and move ahead with all due speed."

Ramble found it hard to disagree with that sentiment. He'd seen more than enough faculty time wasted on long-winded debates concerning matters his colleagues knew little about. He'd despaired as the department voted in favor of one measure or another—often with a minimum of expertise—only to abdicate responsibility for following through the very next day. Theoretically, faculty ought to be great at academic self-government and decision making; in reality, these highly educated citizens sometimes resembled unruly, petulant, irresponsible teenagers. Though in his heart he wished otherwise, Ramble knew a union of the "ought" and "is" seemed farfetched. He'd accepted the department's chair position reluctantly, out of a sense of obligation to his colleagues. But, he did want to make things work out well.

Shafts of sunlight filtered down to bathe the president's face. His wavy dark hair, styled, razor cut, and moussed, cascaded up from a wide brow, dwarfing the rest of his thin and delicate facial profile. His eyes seemed dim and veiled in contrast to what might have been expected from such a gifted rustler of real estate dollars. As he continued voicing his thoughts, Dingkudgel stepped next to Luella. She recoiled from the hand resting on her shoulder as if touched by an aging country club grandee in full golfer's regalia. Dingkudgel seemed unaware of her reaction, his eyes searching the auditorium's heavens.

"In conclusion, allow me the privilege of sharing with all faculty a recent message to department chairs." The president folded his hands on his chest. "I have asked them to be the best of leaders—shepherds leading us toward change and transformation. I have asked them to consider, 'What makes a quality department?' I have asked them, 'How can you help create a culture of excellence?' I now ask them to go forth in search of the best future for faculty, students, departments, and this university. Management by Vision, my friends."

Ramble sure as hell didn't see his role as department chair in such messianic terms. There had to be a better way to achieve some of the worthy goals he glimpsed among the smoke and mirrors conjured by Dingkudgel. But how could he and his department faculty fashion a quality department?

"While I prefer not to begin our school year during such a time of testing," Dingkudgel intoned, "nevertheless, all of us must persevere toward higher goals. It's time for the buy in, my friends. I see before us a future in which, for one thing, we expand our graduate degree curriculum."

Dingkudgel's pronouncement drew unconcealed gasps from the faculty. He then dropped a second bombshell. "I see in that same future vision a top of the line distance learning network, stretching from our humble campus to the corners of the globe." Gasps changed to choking sounds. But the president wasn't finished yet. "I see our university developing athletic teams to compete at an advanced level of competition, allowing our sturdy men and robust young women to test their skills with the best in the nation."

Faculty reaction ranged from shocked silence to loud outcries for and against the president's final whammy.

"Do we have enough steroids?" yelled one outraged professor.

"Do we have a school rouser?" another professor snarled.

"Will there be a marching band?" Guy Lumberto, professor of brass instruments in the music department, seemed positively elated.

"The Fighting Snowmen. That's what to call our teams," August sang out. Luella glared at him.

"Snowpersons?" a chastened August mumbled in return.

Ignoring the tumult he'd created, Dingkudgel stretched out his arms, thrusting his chest forward, silver pins for record-breaking real estate sales on the lapels of his double-breasted pinstripe suit glittering in the spotlight he had contrived. "I propose to this assemblage nothing less than the rebirth of our campus. Each faculty member, each staff member, each departmental chair, and each of the new academic vice presidents I shall hire—all must come aboard this majestic train and travel to the future."

In the middle of a growing murmur of conversations that broke out among the faculty, Ramble overheard colleagues near him trying out rap lyrics. "A new academic veep . . . *a uh a uh* . . . we suspectin' mission creep."

August hummed a chorus of "Chattanooga Choo Choo."

Luella, smiling a wicked smile, contributed a soft version of a song Ramble recognized from an old John Denver album for kids: "Daddy, What's a Train?"

"Wrong way on a one-way track," Soul Asylum's lyric seemed best to Ramble. Alas, it provided little comfort as he considered the university's future.

CHAPTER 4

Ramble decided not to stick around for the last minutes of the assembly. A beautiful fall morning beckoned, so he sneaked out a back exit while the president's aides distributed talking points and FAQs for the Management by Vision plan. The faculty intranet site would have the particulars on what Ramble suspected was a done deal.

The university lay in a hushed, sylvan setting, though not far at all from St. Paul's bustling Midway District and Grand Avenue's growing wealth of shops and restaurants. The campus boasted plenty of open space and gardens; quaint walking paths lined with maples, oaks, and elms; and excellent wooden benches for soaking up the sunshine. Ramble sat on his favorite bench near the student union. From there he could survey the comings and goings of the university community and read the bimonthly campus newspaper.

The welcome-back issue had been put to bed before the weekend, so no mention of Roland Norris's murder appeared. A story with the headline "The New University: Today's College Student" graced the front page and continued inside. Most of the feature dealt with the social and cultural proclivities of the university's students who were now walking the mall and marching up the steps of the student union, but the last few paragraphs held Ramble's interest.

"Like most of their kind throughout the country, Välkommen U students prefer to plot their class schedules to avoid, at all costs, Thursday afternoon and Friday classes. 'Thirstdays,' and 'Horizontal Fridays' are de rigueur for today's college students."

Ramble hadn't paid much attention to that particular campus trend. But now that he thought about it, few students showed up at Välkommen U on Friday mornings. The campus grill didn't even open for breakfast until 10:00 a.m. on Fridays because of the lack of business. Ramble realized that he and a couple of other senior professors in his department were among the few who taught classes on Friday mornings. The whole thing seemed wrong to him—not good for students in particular, and a bad sign to those outside the campus if professors showed up to work only four days a week. Hard-working parents and less-fortunate students squeezing out tuition payments and piling up student loans certainly could take umbrage at a four-day campus workweek. Somebody needed to squelch the problem before it got completely out of hand. Ramble needed to do something as department chair. He admonished himself for letting the issue slip.

The remaining paragraphs of the news article also revealed much about college students that Ramble still found surprising. He didn't know exactly how much students worked these days, and he'd greatly overestimated the hours they devoted to study. Apparently, students across the country now spent more time attending class than studying. How could they work at a job thirty hours and average only ten hours of study a week for a full semester's course load, and yet still end up with high grade point averages? It didn't make sense.

Turning to the last page, Ramble read through the end of the article under the subhead: "We Learn Differently." It sounded like a manifesto.

"As students, we are quite different from our parents' generation in the ways we learn. We are the digital generation of students. As John Seely Brown has suggested, we are 'multiprocessors'—listening to our music, talking on cell phones, and using our portable computers. We do not want to be 'targets of predigested learning,' devoid of emotion, unhooked from the Internet, and without gaming and action."

Looking about the mall, Ramble saw students were indeed "multi-processing." Toes tapped in rhythm with iPods while fingers skipped across the keys of BlackBerrys, iPhones, and laptop computers. Some talked on their cell phones while reading textbooks. They could access the Internet from almost any nook and cranny of the campus thanks to the new Wi-Fi system. Ramble suspected a high percentage were checking out the latest on YouTube and updating their Facebook or Twitter pages. Välkommen U students now had a choice of over a hundred cable TV channels in their dorm rooms. He wondered if students from less-privileged economic backgrounds could fully take part in the digital revolution.

The tone and logic the student newspaper piece adopted favoring the wonders of information technology troubled Ramble. Over the years he'd come to accept what educational researchers believed: Different people learn in different ways. But he wasn't convinced that short bursts of information broadcast through multiple sources helped students learn. From his point of view, drastically lessened spans of attention seemed a more likely outcome of multiprocessing. And the idea of reading texts and books on those newfangled Kindle machines or an iPad made his blood boil. At the least, students needed textbooks and collections of readings—*in books, dammit*—so they could read and learn at some depth. Didn't they?

And reading books and articles as computer downloads? No way.

The article also mentioned something called *swirling*, which Ramble translated as students' taking courses at a variety of institutions, including community colleges and online, all the while enrolled and pursuing their degrees at a home college or university. Too much swirling, Ramble thought, and students wouldn't have a unique educational experience within the environment of a specific campus. Was this an old-fashioned notion?

The writer of the article had no room for negatives, but Ramble could think of several disturbing characteristics of "today's college student." What appeared as a darn near intractable lack of curiosity exhibited by students particularly aggrieved him. He'd grown accustomed to his students' blank looks when asked about a poet, a writer, or a cultural icon. OK, fine, they didn't know Robert Penn Warren from Willa

Cather. But no twinges of regret? No sparks of interest? Ramble caught himself before playing the "in my day" game. Still. . . .

Why had so many students lost their curiosity about what they didn't know? Why didn't they have the motivation to learn about the poets and authors Ramble loved and thought suitable for the ages? Was he just being an old fuddy-duddy?

"Thinking about a next victim, Professor Ramble?" The tall black man standing next to Ramble wore a sharp-looking brown leather jacket over a blue oxford cloth shirt and a pair of trendy denims. In his hand, he held a gold badge for Ramble to see.

"Detective Jarvis." Ramble read the name on the badge. "What can I do for you?"

"Let's talk for a few minutes."

"Do I have a choice?"

"Probably not." Jarvis sat next to Ramble on the bench.

"I guess you heard about some of the disagreements Professor Norris and I had over the years." Ramble should have expected he'd draw suspicion. "You've been talking to some of Roland's little buddies, I guess."

Jarvis shrugged a small notebook out from an inside jacket pocket along with a ballpoint pen.

"I'd have thought these days you guys would be carrying some cell phone thing that did everything but your laundry," Ramble said.

The detective didn't reply, fixing a pleasant smile on his face.

"Is this like psychotherapy? You wait until I need to say something?" Ramble didn't like games much—especially when the deck was stacked against him.

"Is there anything you'd like to *share* with me, Professor Ramble?" Jarvis poised the ballpoint pen over his notepad. He couldn't hold up his end of the joke, and a smile broke across his face.

"Just what I need, a Freudian police detective talking Minnesotan," Ramble said.

Jarvis pretended to be disappointed. "It's been a while since I was in school here."

"When was that?"

"Oh, back in the early days. I used to play noon-hour basketball with you professors."

Ramble took a longer look at the detective. "Sure you did. A nifty move on the baseline, right?"

"That's me."

"Sorry. Didn't recognize you in long pants."

Jarvis pointed his pen at Ramble. "What do you say, Professor, can you help me fill up this notebook and get on with my business?"

"Are you serious?"

"Hmm. Do you think I can be?"

"*Now cut that out!*" Ramble used his best Jack Benny imitation.

Jarvis didn't crack a smile this time. Too young for the *Jack Benny Show*, Ramble guessed.

"All I know is, you and Norris had a history, and it didn't end with little tiffs about liberal arts requirements," Jarvis said.

"We had a few battles, and we didn't get along from day one. Roland was a flaming asshole. But I never got to the point where I contemplated extinguishing him."

"Cute, Professor." Jarvis clicked his ballpoint pen and put it and the notebook back inside his leather jacket. "We'll talk again soon."

CHAPTER 5

"Ready to meet this year's crop of parents?"

Ramble recognized the nasal, whiny voice and tried to wish its owner away. Abel Billings, a former professor of theology who had found salvation in academic administration, slumped against Ramble's office door, a smirk decorating his Mr. Potato Head physiognomy. Billings served as assistant dean and bureaucratic guru for the College of Liberal Arts—setting up class schedules, keeping track of the budget, doing all the nasty paperwork the institution required, and attempting to massage conflicts and complaints before they reached the desk of the soon-to-retire dean, Agnes Sharp. Everyone knew Billings had his sights set on Sharp's administrative post, and making sure academic departments sent representatives to every university meeting and function scheduled throughout the year seemed one way for the aspirant to demonstrate his potential. A busy man was Abel Billings.

The New Parents Meeting fell into the category of early semester functions that few department chairs in the liberal arts area had the slightest inclination to attend. But in exchange for explaining the value of liberal learning each fall semester, the assistant dean allowed Ramble to escape a few committee duties. Ramble saw it as a bargain.

"Remember to stick to the usual script. We may have to revisit it next semester, but it'll keep the parents happy for now." Billings allowed himself another smirk. "Your audience awaits."

"Say hi to all the leadership team on the eighth floor, Abel. Teamwork, baby. Deliver that product."

Ramble watched the departing bureaucrat's retreat. How nice it would be to stuff the little prig into a file drawer. Did tenure allow faculty members one semilethal assault?

Five minutes later, Ramble stood in front of some fifty parents sated with special bag lunches from Quick-Bytes, an off-campus bakery and electronic café. The parents seemed restless, despite the scrumptious white chocolate chip cookies for dessert. Counting frowns and hostile looks, Ramble concluded several of the parents had decided not to go gently into the night. It wasn't only the news of Roland Norris's murder that had unhinged them. Most likely they hadn't yet forgotten their visit to the Bursar's Office where their checkbooks took a sizable hit for tuition and dormitory fees. Not the most opportune moment to launch into a spiel about the liberal arts perhaps. Had the parents been to the bookstore yet? As Ramble settled in at the podium, a loud voice cut through the murmur of conversations.

"Hey, Professor. Before you start, let me ask you a little question."

Ramble scanned the right side of the room and located the questioner, a thick-necked guy, sprawled back in a chair, a cup of coffee balanced on a large belly not quite covered by a bright orange polo shirt. Next to him sat a woman with thin, curly brown hair who seemed ready to bolt and run in a second.

"Ask away." Ramble tried his best to set a welcoming look on his face.

"It says in your university catalog that my kid has to take a whole bunch of courses in the liberal arts at the expense of his career interests. I'm hoping you've got something to say that'll convince me all this stuff is worth it. I'm forking out a ton of money for tuition if you know what I mean." The man jutted his jaw forward and turned to the audience, waving the catalog above his head. He brushed the woman's warning hand off his forearm and wiggled the fingers of his free hand like a poker player waiting for Ramble to ante up. "Enlighten us, Professor. Aren't these liberal arts courses . . . um—"

"I suspect the gentleman is searching for the word *abstract*." A well-fed, slightly balding man dressed in a classy three-piece suit smiled at Ramble. He sat at a table reserved for members of the university Advisory Board—a collection of business and corporate types, peppered with local politicians and a few community representatives. "If I am hearing correctly what this gentleman said, he's asking for something more down to earth than the rhetoric one reads in the college catalog."

The college faculty representatives and admissions staff seated behind Ramble exhaled covertly, obviously thankful he had the lead role in the proceedings. Ramble imagined himself in his easy chair, taking that first sip of a strong bourbon Manhattan and stroking his dog's silky coat. It had been a long day already, and Ramble needed to be back early the next morning for a department meeting. He had to admit too that Detective Jarvis's veiled accusations about the murder had thrown him off stride. Ramble walked to a spot near the guy in the orange shirt who'd asked the first question.

"Maybe the word this gentleman is searching for is *inessential*," Ramble said. "Maybe, it's *highfalutin'*."

"How about *la-di-da*." The guy smiled broadly at Ramble. The woman, most likely his wife, studied the rim of her coffee cup. Others in the room nodded and murmured in support. Hadn't Ramble read somewhere that most Americans suspected not higher education but the high school system for the failure of their sons' and daughters' educations? So much for the latest surveys.

"I think I understand why as a parent I might feel the same way." Ramble looked at both of his interrogators, hoping to establish a polite connection. "These are tough economic times, and college tuition and expenses aren't cheap."

A woman in corporate getup and starched blonde hair called out, "One of my daughters graduated from here five years ago. I may be reading the requirements wrong, but it looks like the number of courses offered to fulfill the liberal education requirements has increased quite a bit. Is this true?"

"Yes. That's correct," Ramble admitted, knowing that the number of courses students could select from for general education and liberal education components looked like the Google search results for Tiger Woods and Paris Hilton combined.

"Yet, you've reduced the total number of required credits for liberal education."

"That's true."

The woman wrinkled her brow and stared at Ramble. "I don't get it."

Ramble could understand her frustration. He shared it. About every five years the campus would gear up for a revision of the liberal learning component of the BA degree. The departments engaged in an odd path of decision making—usually snipping off the total number of liberal learning credits from degree requirements but then engaging in a mad and destructive scramble to ramp up the number of courses eligible to fulfill the reduced requirements. In Ramble's experience, the process seldom included any thoughtful investigation of the role of the liberal arts in an undergraduate education or any meaningful evidence on why a student ought to take courses in the specific required areas. Did a student actually benefit in some measurable way from the imposed curriculum? Strip away all the rhetoric, and the bottom line was that the departments needed the enrollments and the exposure to haul in future majors. More elective courses—that was the answer for many. Perfect a few solid course choices? Cooperate? Construct interdisciplinary courses focused on the fundamental understandings and skills? Uh-uh. Ramble knew all about the under-the-table deals and horse trading practiced by the departments with all the spirit and cunning of the worst politicos. He'd fought a losing rear guard action for his department the last time around. Välkommen U faculty found a way to expand the curriculum by widening the definition of a "shared common knowledge" to include a host of courses without the slightest connection to the original intent of general education and liberal learning. It seemed to be all about departmental boodle.

"In essence, the choices of how to fulfill the requirements have increased. So, yes, there are more courses. I regret the trend." Ramble was damn well not going to defend the faculty's decision making on that score. He glanced up at the clock. Still a half hour before he could send everyone off for a financial reckoning at the bookstore.

A woman at the same table as the previous questioner pushed aside the remains of her lunch to signal a serious intent. She adjusted a pair of reading glasses on the tip of her nose and scanned a page of the university's catalog. Ramble feared another bullet aimed at his vital organs.

"What is the difference, pray tell, among these terms—general education, liberal education, and the liberal arts?"

Ramble cocked an eyebrow and smiled his best smile. "Do you have an hour or so?" What used to work on his mother now failed miserably. *So long, boyish charm.*

"I hope you can explain it to the students." The woman seemed satisfied having made her point and poured herself a stream of hot coffee from the insulated carafe on her table.

To be honest, Ramble did find the terminology in the catalog confusing, not to mention frustrating and embarrassing, especially if students were asked to join in the whole sorry business without foreknowledge and enthusiasm. General education? Sure. It's "part of a liberal education curriculum shared by all students, providing broad exposure to multiple disciplines and forming the basis for developing important intellectual and civic capacities." That's what the glossy print informed readers. Yada, yada, yada. So what?

"I think it's clear we need to do a better job explaining ourselves to students and parents." As Ramble made an admission of collective university guilt, he noticed none other than President Dingkudgel and Dean Sharp standing by the dining room's main door. Maybe he'd quell the parents' rising hostility by introducing the administrative pair and shoving them in the spotlight.

"I think explaining the difference between the terms is the least of your problems." Mr. Three-Piece Suit again. His name tag read, "Mr. Bruce Haney."

"Professor, you can explain a liberal education and the liberal arts these days until you're blue in the face," Haney said. "Most people have no use for such fluff. My little corner of the world certainly doesn't."

Just my damn luck, thought Ramble. *The* Bruce Haney, CEO of the mammoth Hiawatha Real Estate and Development Company and chairman of the Minnehaha Foundation—a new wellspring of big grant bucks in the Twin Cities. Haney's "little corner of the world." *Ha*. Hadn't President Dingkudgel mentioned something about that in his welcome letter? Yes. The university had applied for $1.5 million smackers in matching grant monies for outdoor sculptures and other enhancements for the university's campus grounds. How Dingkudgel planned to come up with contingent matching funds from already oversubscribed alumni had baffled the faculty. Ramble recalled that Haney had been one of the financial backers for Dingkudgel's Gopher Valley project years before. That past relationship probably accounted for Haney's appointment to the university's Board of Regents. Maybe he would put the touch on fellow corporate bigwigs in the Twin Cities for matching funds.

Though he nearly gagged saying it, Ramble ventured the company line in response to Haney. "Well the university is, shall we say, well positioned to help students acquire the benefits of a liberal education. Some 80% of our faculty have a PhD or its equivalent in their fields, and as you probably know many of those professors are actively engaged in research and publication and creative endeavors."

Haney seemed unmoved by the "well positioned" thing. Maybe they didn't say things like that in the boardroom anymore. Ramble noticed Angela standing near the doorway. She pretended to stick a finger down her throat. Ramble changed course. "We also have a very active and well-supported faculty development program to help us be better teachers and advisors." With those words, Ramble drew a smile from Angela. She had a nice smile.

Haney didn't. The CEO had a world-class scowl.

"In my business," he said, "if I judged my potential success only on investment or input of capital, would that guarantee my product would be a winner?"

Judging by the knit eyebrows and side conversations among the parents in the audience, Haney had Ramble backpedaling. What's more, Ramble didn't disagree entirely with Haney's analysis—although the businessman's idea of "product" was likely quite different from Ramble's.

"You make a good point," Ramble said.

Haney finally smiled. A victory smile for marketplace wisdom, Ramble assumed.

"I'm not questioning theoretical rationalizations for the liberal arts or the requirements selected," Haney said. "It would be hard to do since I join the majority in this room who have no idea what you mean in your publications. But beyond the rationale and, excuse me, the rhetoric about the value of the liberal arts, what's taking place in the courses and how they are taught seems pretty important. What proof have we that good things occur? Are the various departments engaged in these required courses working together for a final product?"

Ouch. Ramble wanted to get off the mat and score a few points for the home team no matter how suspect his teammates were, but Haney beat him to the punch. The executive pointed out the window nearest his table. "In the real world out there, Professor, we like concrete answers and specific illustrations. The more the better."

Heads in the audience bobbed up and down. Whose side was this guy on? Ramble felt himself growing hot under the collar. Twice mad in the same day? Not a good thing.

"I think our faculty ought to revisit often what our liberal arts requirements mean in that real world of yours Mr. Haney," Ramble said. "We should be ready to give good examples and real experiences to our students. They need to understand why study in the liberal arts is valuable as an ideal, and they need to see why it's useful in your corner of the world. When we require these courses for graduation and set out a system of general education for our students, we should never lose sight of this question: What is an educated person? We should take it seriously and think of it as we construct course learning outcomes and teaching strategies. Our students and their professors need to be mindful of exact and concrete examples of how a liberal education makes a difference in the civic, personal, and the career contexts of our lives." Ramble had stressed the last category. "You want employees who can be something other than entry-level fodder, don't you? You want employees who can analyze situations and not just follow orders, don't you? How about some who write well? I'd venture—and the research indicates—that liberal learning is an important staging ground for future leaders in management and in the so-called real world." Ramble gave his antagonist a good stare. "But I'm just a literature professor."

"Excuse me." One of the mothers across the room interrupted. "I think we're straying off the path here. If my son and his friends are any indication, I find it hard to see these requirements making much impact. I doubt many kids coming out of high school, my son included, have ever heard of a liberal education, much less thought seriously about being an educated person."

Out of the corner of his vision, Ramble noticed President Dingkudgel walking toward him. Ramble wanted to respond to the woman's point. It was a good one. Dingkudgel joined Ramble at the podium, smiling broadly at the audience. "I've had a chance to follow this excellent discussion, and I'm impressed with what I've heard." The president placed his arm around Ramble's shoulder, drawing him close like the pair had been best buddies since grade school.

"Thanks to this wonderful group of parents and our distinguished board member, Mr. Bruce Haney, the administration and faculty of this great university have received our marching orders for this semester. I can't imagine a better person to head a task force than Professor Ramble."

The president released his grip on Ramble. He held the edges of the podium with both hands, leaning forward in a stance that bespoke seriousness, intent, leadership—an iffy personification of the university's original but somewhat suspect motto: Audio Video Disco. Since assuming his presidency, and after an online session with an English-to-Latin Web site, Dingkudgel had persuaded the Board of Deciders to approve a slight change. The university motto now read: Audio Video Disco Animadverto Do. The president apparently had his mind on an upcoming accreditation visit and a downturn in alumni giving. Ramble had doubts if anyone with a whit of study in Latin had contributed to either version of the motto, but the athletic department, the university cheerleading squad, and the Interfraternity Council exulted in the change. It looked much better on sweatshirts and mugs. A member of Eta Mu Pi told the student newspaper: "I think the parents will like it. They used to do stuff like that." As one faculty wag commented to Ramble, "Well, we don't teach Latin anymore, and it's all Greek to them anyway."

"The light of your judgment has shown us a clear path," Dingkudgel continued, gazing with fondness at the audience as he raised his hands skyward. Ramble stepped away from the president feeling like some banished sinner. "We shall reexamine our core purposes of education at this institution to discover the most important educational paths for our students. We will expand their opportunities beyond the classroom by embracing technology, by extending their educational horizons beyond graduation, by testing them on the fields of play. In so doing, mothers and fathers of our precious students, we shall provide answers to the questions put here today with such concern and brilliance."

Dingkudgel lowered his head and clasped his hands together. Ramble heard another collective intake of breath from the faculty representatives.

Ramble glanced at Haney. The corporate heavy hitter seemed much amused.

CHAPTER 6

The Following Day

Ramble took stock of the students packing into the classroom for his introductory American literature course: a bunch of wet-behind-the-ears recent refugees from Minnesota small towns and local high schools as far as he could tell. They horsed around and carried on loud conversations. A scattering of adult students seated near the front of the room looked uncomfortable and out of place. A couple of the women gawked as a young coed walked by wearing a flimsy lace camisole and low-slung, butt-baring jeans. Ramble averted his gaze, busying himself with the class registration list.

"Good morning, my friends." Ramble held up a stack of three-by-five-inch cards and asked a young man in the front row to distribute one to each student. "I never liked classes where the professor didn't know my name, so I'll plan to know each and every one of yours as soon as I can."

Ramble again surveyed the crop of introductory literature novitiates. Only a few seemed excited by the prospect of the class. As he walked the room, passing out his syllabus of three pages, he remembered the days when a page and a half seemed excessive. He understood the reasoning behind a more extensive version, but one young professor in the department had constructed a twenty-pager. He called it a "teaching syllabus." What the hell was that all about? Some of the syllabi faculty put together these days could double as an auto loan contract. Ramble figured if you plunked all the stuff out on paper like a user's manual, how would you ever back up and head in another direction if things went sour in class? What if you or the students had a good new idea?

A bunch of guys attired in variations of black—raincoats, T-shirts, jeans, and polished steel-toed shoes—populated one of the tables near the back of the classroom. Only the streaks of purple, red, or chartreuse in their hair relieved the gloom cast by their outfits and pale faces. Most seemed preoccupied with playing handheld computer games. Ramble eyed a stringy-haired kid wearing a Rolling Stones' red tongue T-shirt. He seemed older, more schooled in the ways of the world—the clothes and hair like a disguise. Concealing what? The student plucked a syllabus from those Ramble had placed on the table and laughed. He flipped the document to the side.

Throughout his teaching life, Ramble treasured any students who made a transition from unfinished ugly ducklings to sparkling personalities by the end of the term. Hardly as many metamorphoses now as before, but those precious few meant something to him. It took some academic tough love, though. Ramble had felt the need in the last few years to remind students who was in charge of the class. It wasn't a stance he adopted easily, but his choices seemed limited.

Like the author of the article he'd read in the student newspaper, Ramble considered many of the students populating his classroom in recent years a different breed. He admitted that might be a bit harsh, perhaps nostalgic, but an increasing number of undergraduates armed with cell phones, iPods, mini computers, and who-knows-what-else technological could disrupt classes and seemed to embody what experts called "classroom incivility." Rude? Many seemed to act that way. As the tagline for an article Ramble had read in *The Chronicle of Higher Education* suggested, maybe students needed "Remedial Civility Training." He could count at least ten students texting madly on their cell phones. That craze drove him up the wall. He had an overpowering urge to walk out of the room and keep doing so until the frenzied-fingered students got the message. Add a Walmart-consumer mentality about a college education plus an alarming lack of basic writing and reading skills from many students' K–12 experience, and Ramble felt he had little choice except to lay down the law. At least that was his first reaction to what he observed in this particular class.

He read to the class from a short section in the syllabus he'd labeled, "Your Academic Protocol." He'd picked a friendly, cheerful font for that section. It didn't take long for the expected question.

"What's *protocol*, Professor Ramble?" A pudgy young man in a grimy, backward baseball cap jabbed his finger at the word on the first page of the syllabus.

"I'm so happy you asked." Ramble stood in front of the student's table. "Where would you find out what protocol means?"

"The dictionary, sir?"

"*Exactamundo.*" Ramble smiled widely and the student joined him. "Everyone in the class will be expected to look up unfamiliar words in a dictionary. In addition, as you see listed under number four, I don't particularly like ball caps in my classroom. I know it's picky, but I'm old-fashioned in this regard."

Ramble pointed his finger in rapid succession at the five or so hat-backward boys in the classroom. They stared back in disbelief and grumbled among themselves but slowly removed their caps, some attempting to smooth down prickly hat hair.

Ramble ran through some of his pet peeves, from cell phones and texting to arriving late for class to food and beverage consumption. The majority of students looked straight ahead—listless, sullen, acting as if they'd heard it all too many times before. Maybe they had, Ramble thought. "I'm just trying to put together some ground rules so we can enjoy the wonders of literature," he told the students, adding what he felt to be a friendly lilt to his voice.

He could imagine what older students returning to college thought about what they witnessed in their classes. He'd be thinking like they were. What the hell? Why did a professor waste time highlighting a syllabus, much less creating a long list of behavioral dos and don'ts? "Is this for real?" Ramble overheard a whisper behind him.

"Hell, yeah," came the answer. "My math professor did the same thing in first hour."

In the next few minutes, Ramble tried to win them over with his comedy routine on stupid cell phone conversations ("Yeah . . . I just finished breakfast and I'm going into the science building. I had the cinnamon raisin bagel like yesterday."). In the middle of Ramble's best bit, the classroom door pushed open. A member of the Goth contingent arriving late strode through the door in pink Converse sneakers, black jeans, and a matching tight jersey shirt, arms encased in sets of odd bracelets, a nose ring flashing, an L.A. Raiders cap worn at an angle over her boyish haircut, and a cell phone glued to her ear.

All eyes shifted to Ramble.

"Hi. Welcome to class. Your arrival comes at a particularly apt moment."

The young woman stopped on her way to the table reserved by the look-alike crew, cell phone conversation suspended in midwhisper. "Can you give the class the benefit of your opinion on what we were just discussing?" Ramble asked his question in a gentle voice, smiling. He didn't have it in mind to be mean or overbearing.

The student switched off her cell phone and eyed the professor. "Let's see . . . Was it the *Scarlet Letter?*"

"Well, as you'll discover when we read Hawthorne, your sin is not so deep," Ramble said, smiling again. "Please arrive for class on time, would you? Thanks."

The student gave Ramble a sour look and made a beeline for the seat her friends had reserved for her. The kid in the Rolling Stones shirt wrote something on a sheet of paper, circulating it to his comrades at the table.

"Professor, sir?" The student questioner wore a black sweatshirt cut off at the shoulders to expose well-muscled arms that looked as big as a normal man's thighs. He had two elaborate arrows tattooed on his biceps, pointing toward meaty hands. T. D. Swenson. Ramble knew him from the press he'd received as a high school football star in St.

Paul. This young stud must be the vanguard of recruiting for Välkommen U's projected future as a football power. Like many of the athletes, T. D. had spent his freshman year tuning up his game and his "academics" at a private community college specializing in such things, located somewhere in western Kansas. Good lord, Ramble thought, we really are on the road to big-time college athletics. Ramble didn't wish to prejudge, but he imagined the stout lad's tattoos might be a necessary coaching aid.

"How come you don't let us wear hats in class?" T. D. touched the brim of a well-worn Vikings cap to emphasize his question.

"Naturally, I have no legal right to exclude the wearing of headgear in my class, Mr. Swenson."

"T. D. don't be wearing no headgear." The future NFL first-rounder rubbed a huge hand through a stubble of blond hair. He grinned. "That'd be silly." He held up his ratty looking Vikings' cap. "We talking 'bout T. D.'s lucky lid, Professor."

A student behind Ramble whispered to a friend, "How does a 245-pound Norwegian dude get to rapping like that?"

"It may sound silly," Ramble said, "but in my class I choose to have students aspire to the highest of their learning abilities. To do so, they should see the classroom as something other than a run-of-the-mill place."

"T. D. not talking 'bout Hurricane Katrina." The "Norse Kamikaze," a moniker the Twin Cities' sportswriters also favored for the young football whiz, plopped the faded Vikings cap back on his massive cranium and brought the brim backward with a deft twist.

"Let's talk about grading, then." Ramble didn't intend to back down and pointed to the second page of the syllabus, looking directly at T. D. Grades still mattered, Ramble assumed. Within a proper interval necessary to preserve his image, T. D. removed his cap. Point taken, apparently.

A young woman raised her hand. "Professor. I have a question?"

"Go ahead."

"Will this class give me something I can *really* use once I graduate?" The student tapped her finger on the syllabus before her. A prim little thing, she was smartly dressed in comparison to her classmates, with makeup applied in a careful but prominent display. Ramble imagined she might be ready for a turn behind an upscale department store jewelry counter. Only an agitated tic of her thin polished lips detracted from the outward display of fashion.

"You've posed an excellent question," Ramble said. One that he expected many a student had in mind these days. "It's a fair question, too."

Several students rolled their eyes and made nasty asides to their friends without bothering to whisper. The young woman sat poised at her table, ignoring the rising commotion around her, sharp blue eyes fixed on Ramble, a steady clicking of burnished nails on her plastic notebook cover demanding a response she would no doubt dispute.

Ramble signaled for a couple of students at a table near the back to calm down and listen. He walked near where they sat and asked, "It's a good question, don't you think?" He waited for an answer, searching the students' faces.

The young woman continued her fingernail rat-a-tat.

Ramble felt a tinge of anger rising. He didn't want to lose his temper on the first day of class. How not to do so?

He heard one of the students expel an angry sigh. "Just tell her to shut up."

"So what did you do?" Angela wore a pair of reading glasses, and she peered over the lenses at Ramble. He'd dropped by her office after class.

"I didn't get angry."

"That's good. So how did the great professor control his impulse and save the day?"

"I went to the texts."

"Meaning?"

"The majority of the students this very evening will be attending to the question: 'What does my favorite work of literature teach me about life?' And for extra credit: 'Should it?' "

Angela turned back to the folder of papers on her desk. "I can't wait to hear about some of the selections in the category of "my favorite work of literature."

"Yes. There is that." Ramble hadn't thought that far ahead. Maybe he'd be pleasantly surprised. He really hoped so.

"Would you like to make some guesses over dinner sometime?" Ramble thought he sounded sufficiently casual in asking his question, despite the beating of his heart.

"You're on, Professor."

CHAPTER 7

Ramble headed across campus to the student union after a workout at the recreation center. The day had not gone well, he lamented. He owed himself a treat. The soft drink dispenser at the Campus Grille held several different flavors and lots of tiny ice cubes. He grabbed a 16-ounce cup, filled it three quarters full with diet cola, and topped it off with some lime-flavored beverage. The smell of freshly baked cookies wafted from the Kookie Krumbles Kounter. Where was Edd Byrnes when you needed him?

At the checkout counter, Ramble glanced beyond the cashier at the remodeled eating area. In one of the 1950s-style retro booths, replete with spanking new cushy red leather benches and black Formica table-tops, two familiar figures sat with a small group of students—the same kids who'd been in Ramble's intro class. He recognized the student with the Rolling Stones T-shirt. What was his name? Norman something . . . Norman Cady. That was it. He wasn't one of the eighteen-to twenty-two-year-old aggregate. Cady looked like he might be several years older. Short and wiry, with solid muscles stretching his T-shirt, a dark, ugly-looking dragon tattoo across the back of his neck, Cady seemed like a first-class troublemaker to Ramble.

Ivars Iverson and Professor Hiram T. Ecker didn't notice Ramble's approach. A fancy handheld electronic gizmo held their attention. Ivars's stubby fingers flew across the game buttons manipulating some odd-looking creature on the small screen chasing others toward a spaceship.

Hiram growled encouragement. "Shoot the little cretins, Ivars."

A linebacker on Ramble's college football team, Ivars didn't look much like the bulldog tackler he'd been in those days of undergraduate gridiron glory. He'd lost weight, and his skin had a sallow tinge. Word had it he'd joined with an odd crew of like-minded professors and students who stayed up all hours role-playing virtual characters in cyberspace. Ivars's strained, sleep-deprived eyes confirmed the rumored addiction.

After a tour in the navy, apparently ending with some trouble, Ivars knocked around the Twin Cities for a time not doing much. Then he seemed to turn things around, enrolling in graduate school to study for an MA in mathematics. He finished his degree and wanted to move on for the PhD but ran out of money after a nasty divorce. The job market stank, but he did manage to catch on part-time at Välkommen U teaching the occasional introductory class and tutoring students. He seemed doomed to the perpetual role of adjunct part-time instructor.

Hiram Ecker taught medieval history. He'd been around since the beginning years of Välkommen U, and Ramble didn't much care for him. A political ideologue and constant scold, Hiram alienated most of his colleagues from day one. Ramble noticed that in recent years Hiram had retreated into a half world composed of his research and fascination with the technology of teaching. But he could always be counted on as a renegade when it came to departmental and university decision making.

Ivars finished the game with a flourish and passed it to one of the students with an appreciative grunt. Not one of the students, except for Norman Cady, gave Ramble the slightest notice as he stepped next to their table. Cady narrowed his eyes and smirked. Hiram saw Ramble, but offered no greeting. He left to get a cup of coffee.

"Ramble." Ivars pushed up the bill of a rumpled red baseball cap. "Still keeping the English Department above board?"

"Always trying, Ivars. You taking care?"

"Same old, same old. Living the life of a poor, part-time faculty member here at this great institution of higher learning."

Ramble knew Ivars barely scraped by with the money he earned from his adjunct teaching. He also picked up some spare change as the on-site janitor in the dumpy student apartment building where he lived. Probably didn't have any health insurance. He rode a beat-up bike everywhere around campus.

"You teaching math again this semester?" Ramble heard there had been talk of hiring a part-time assistant professor.

"I'm down to one night course and tutoring now." Ivars eyed a plate of French fries and Cokes the students had ordered. "I'm hoping for a surge of late registration so they'll open up some new sections. All those years they needed someone to pick up the extra classes, and now they can't find a section for me. No one thought to ask me to apply for the half-time slot."

"That doesn't sound right." Ramble couldn't do anything more than offer a shot of sympathy.

"Things may be looking up, though," Ivars said. "Yes, indeed. Some changes are coming."

"Some new teaching opportunities?" Ramble knew that most of the local colleges and universities were adding adjuncts, especially to cover lower-level required courses for majors or general education.

"Nothing like that," Ivars said. "Something better."

"That sounds great. You want to join me for a sandwich? My treat."

"Don't need the charity, Ramble."

"I wasn't offering any."

"Forget it." Ivars took back the handheld game from the student sitting next to him. He fingered the keyboard. "Did you know that almost 50% of faculty now are part-timers? It's Walmart comes to campus, you know. Work hard, do a good job, and don't expect any benefits. At least they give you a uniform and a discount on products at the real thing."

"I know it's not right, Ivars." Ramble had kept the use of adjuncts to the minimum in his department, but the pressure was on to have more appointments off the tenure track. He tried to look out for the adjunct appointments in his department, especially by including them in department activities and providing the best possible in professional development possibilities. It wasn't much. He'd made it a personal commitment to lobby for better compensation.

"At least with those yearly contracts, I felt like I was different, maybe had a little niche. Now that I'm a bottom-feeder, you guys on the top look real fat and tasty."

"I'll keep that in mind." Ramble felt uneasy around Ivars these days—less sorry for him than before. He seemed a bit unhinged. Life as an adjunct could do that, Ramble suspected.

"Now I'm reading that we're to blame for *your* students not being successful." Ivars gave Ramble an angry look. "Sorry, but just because the freshman students I teach around here don't get all sorts of extra time and care from me isn't my damn fault. I'm not getting paid for the extras."

Hiram Ecker eased back into the booth. His reddish goatee and long sideburns contrasted with a growing bald spot edging toward complete coverage of his skull. He looked like a peasant straight out of a Thomas Hardy novel, with thick forearms and a short, husky upper body. His red T-shirt bore the inscription Authority Sucks!

"I thought you'd be into blogging or something by now, Hiram, not fooling with these handheld kids' games," Ramble said.

"You'd be surprised about gaming." Hiram glanced at the students working their handheld devices. "Lots more to it than meets the eye."

"Get with the times, Ramble," Ivars said. "You might learn something."

Ramble figured it was time to leave and didn't see the need to say good-bye.

Ivars, Hiram, and all but one of the students bent over their electronic games with determination. Cady allowed Ramble a hard look, sizing him up, like some newbie in a cell block.

"See you in class, Ace." Ramble said.

Cady offered no reply.

CHAPTER 8

The Following Morning

"Meet Nadine Watkins. She's one of our candidates for African American studies."

Sam Agee, chair of the African American studies program, stood next to a petite woman attired in a dark blue linen suit, crisp white blouse, and as close to sensible shoes as any definition would allow. Ramble recognized the woman's friendly smile and eyes filled with resolve. She'd been one of his students.

"Professor Ramble. It's so nice to see you again."

"New Voices in American Literature . . . about seven years ago?"

"Yes. I was Nadine Henderson then. I didn't graduate from here. I finished at the U of M."

Ramble had no idea his former student was one of the several candidates for the African American studies position. As a last-minute replacement on the hiring committee, Ramble had only a few minutes the night before to review Nadine's application letter and curriculum vitae. He felt bad for it but didn't have much choice given Norris's murder and the opening of classes. He remembered Nadine as an excellent student. He should have made the connection after glancing at her application.

"I need to get our committee members in here," Sam informed Nadine, patting her shoulder like a father.

Sam was one of only two African Americans on the Välkommen U faculty. The other, Kwami Abada, a political scientist, held a half-time appointment. Ramble knew his colleague and friend had fought long and hard to establish African American studies, and Sam wanted the program to continue after he retired. He faced a determined opposition once led by Roland Norris. "If I leave without a replacement," he told Ramble, "Kwami will be the only one left standing in our academic ghetto. I'm afraid African American studies will lose out if I can't hire additional faculty."

President Dingkudgel had agreed about hiring someone for a new position, but Ramble guessed the president had different motives for that decision from Sam's. Pressured by a university and a citizen's committee to hire another African American faculty member, Dingkudgel declared Välkommen U would move forward to become "more diverse" and encompass significant "communities of ethnicity" within the Twin Cities. He didn't mention the African American studies program in his statement.

Earlier that summer, Sam and Ramble stopped by the Purple Onion on Snelling Avenue for a late afternoon pizza and a couple of drinks. Sam talked about what he thought the administration's plans might be. "They'll add this one position now to keep Black students coming here from the cities, but what they've got in mind is quite different. They don't like African American studies by itself as a program, and they're figuring out how to eliminate it." Sam slammed his hand down, juggling the steins of beer. "I'm ready to fight."

Ramble rarely had seen Sam lose his temper, despite several noteworthy provocations over all the years. Most of the faculty—liberal and conservative alike—didn't take African American studies programs seriously according to what Ramble heard around the campus. Liberals talked a good game and said the right things. Conservatives were less tentative about the matter. For a variety of reasons, many faculty members remained silent. Ramble knew Sam felt isolated and on the defensive. Despite energetic research and several publications, he received little praise from the university community. Some faculty members, especially Roland Norris and his cronies, let it be known they didn't consider Sam's work to be of great consequence. Norris's cabal found it difficult to eliminate the African American studies program but worked to keep it at the edges of the mainstream curriculum.

"If I don't get someone good, full of fight, African American studies will end up as some watered-down monument to—hell, I don't know what." Sam took a long pull on his beer. "We've always had important things to say to students as a field of study, and we still do. I'll be damned if we'll end up as nothing more than a strategy to attract Black students and to make sure the university looks good by having a few faculty of color."

Ramble figured the recent, sizable population increase of African immigrants and the established Asian and Chicano/a-Latino/a communities of the Twin Cities presaged a new ethnic studies program in the minds of administrators and others at the university—one incorporating African American studies.

"I've got some theories," Sam said. "I can see why the administrators like the idea of ethnic studies for upping enrollments and protecting their ass on equal opportunity. I can even understand why our good-hearted liberal faculty members think pitching an all-encompassing ethnic studies tent is a positive step. I think many of them like that diversity ideal, immigrants as Horatio Alger—all that stuff. Makes it easier for them to swallow than leftover chunks of homegrown racial injustice and underrepresentation."

Ramble took a slice of pizza and offered some to his friend, wondering if another round of beers might be in order. Sam waved off the suggestion. "I'm just getting going, Jack. Listen. A few years from now, African American studies might be so far out on the margins, we could yell 'fire' and nobody will pay any attention." Sam traced circles on the table surface. "So the university will end up with a gold star for promoting diversity and marginalize a program they don't like at the same time."

Ramble wondered if things were that simple. Sam sometimes laid it on Ramble a little thick, just to keep him thinking. "Sam, are you being too conspiratorial?"

"We'll see."

"What are the chances you can hire someone as tough and ornery as you?"

"Few and little." Sam smiled and drained his beer. "But this here trickster rabbit has a few surprises left."

"Thump your tail for another round?"

Sam smiled for the first time in their conversation. "I'll hop if you'll pop."

"I'm glad you're on the list of candidates." Ramble opened up his folder to Nadine's curriculum vitae. "This is impressive. You did a great job in graduate school."

"But you're wondering why I'm applying here at Välkommen U."

"I can't deny it." Ramble steered the young woman to a corner of the conference room. "It looks like you have a nice situation where you are."

Nadine gave Ramble a look he remembered from her student days. She often called him to account for his interpretations of the novels they read. She never did so on reflex. Nadine always began with the text and used her experience and perspective to turn Ramble and the class to a different interpretive page. Teacher and student didn't always agree, but Ramble learned much from their discussions.

"I'm missing something again?"

"Maybe we can talk after the interview," Nadine said. "I'll have a few minutes before meeting with the dean."

Renée Forbes, chair of the faculty committee on diversity, gave Ramble a curt nod as she sat down in the remaining open chair next to him.

"Looks like we have a good prospect," Ramble said.

Renée ignored Ramble's comment, intent on organizing papers she withdrew from her briefcase. Renée's personality could best be described as prickly. She had a habit of taking everything way too seriously, Ramble thought, and rarely seemed to take any pleasure in her work. Ramble's interactions with her were sporadic at best, so maybe she had another personality—brimming with warmth and wit, carefully reserved for an exciting, though well-concealed off-campus life.

Today she wore her hair pulled back in a tight bun, with only a pair of lonely silver earrings as accompaniment.

To start off the session, as requested of all candidates, Nadine was to present a twenty-minute class session typical of how she would teach an introductory African American studies course. She had a surprise ready for the committee. Without preface, Nadine launched into a brilliant summary of her research on images of slavery in the works of civil rights–era novelists and poets. Ramble thought she would be a top candidate at any university.

"That was a most unexpected presentation Ms. Watkins. Most articulate. But I must inquire—did you misunderstand the purpose of our request for a teaching preview?"

Professor Briney Sweatman, one of Roland Norris's former retinue, a pudgy, jowly guy with a drinker's red speckled nose, fluffed his paisley tie and avoided looking at Nadine, addressing his question to the opposite wall. A quick exchange of glances between Nadine and Sam Agee suggested Sweatman had stepped over a line.

Sam had circulated an article on the subject of racial microaggressions to the faculty the past week. Sweatman had read the article and turned it to his own purposes. If Ramble recalled correctly, everyday conversations, social behaviors, and places—like a predominantly white Välkommen University campus—provided the right circumstances for indignities practiced against African Americans, Asian Americans, and other groups. These indignities could best be described as nasty, insulting, discrediting, negative, and disparaging racial remarks and incivilities. The kicker in it all was that the microaggressions could be intended, like Sweatman's, or unintentional. An example of the latter category that stuck in Ramble's mind had to do with a Latina student appearing for a computer technology job interview and the interviewer saying something like, "Oh, *you're* Anita?" Whether inadvertent or not, the cumulative affect of racial microaggressions had serious consequences. Ramble cringed at the thought of college students carrying about what the social scientists described as *racial battlefield fatigue*. On the positive side, Nadine Watkins seemed quite capable of winning any battle. So Ramble held tight to his basic impulses with regard to Sweatman's pain-in-the-butt behavior.

"I felt the substance of my candidacy might best be . . . articulated . . . by introducing my scholarly direction, Professor Sweatman." Nadine smiled sweetly at her interrogator. "As I believe you might agree, a fundamental basis of good teaching is scholarship in a field."

Nadine defanged Sweatman using the same argument he employed so often over the years in denouncing faculty development expenditures for teaching seminars. He had no comeback at the ready and sank back into his chair, sullen and brooding, but not finished causing trouble if Ramble could read his face. Ramble stole a glance at Sam, whose eyes left no doubt of his delight about the turn of events. And Nadine wasn't done yet.

"If I am to be hired here," she said, "I would ask that you grant me a joint appointment in the literature department. I think doing so would help dispel some misconceptions—which I hope do not hold at this institution—that African American studies and its faculty members are only specialized adjuncts to the established university curricula."

Ramble noted with pleasure that once again Nadine delivered her message in a voice as calm and sweet as a mourning dove. Several committee members near Ramble whispered among themselves, frowns and worry clouding their faces at the developing confrontation. Ramble guessed Sweatman was happy to go on the offensive. But before he could fire off an initial volley, Harlene Jenkins, a committee member from chemistry with a reputation for asking the implausible question at the most inappropriate moments, called for Nadine's "laptop policy."

"It is problematic, isn't it?" Nadine looked intently at Harlene. "I ran into this quite a bit last year. Almost every student at my university has a laptop, and most of them bring it along to class. In fact, the university encouraged it."

"So what did you do?" Ramble knew Harlene had already made up her mind on the issue long ago; she'd gone digital.

"I hesitate to provide a hard and fast solution, because I think it depends on the situation," Nadine said.

Harlene's thin bloodless lips twisted into a tight line. "Yes, yes. But what did you do?"

"I talked with my students about appropriate times to use their laptops, but I put in a lot of effort reviewing my course to ensure most class sessions guaranteed students would be working on problems and discussing them. I felt my teaching should be about student engagement and active learning." Despite Harlene's obvious disagreement, signaled by a barely disguised hissing sound, Nadine stuck to her guns. "I judge part of my teaching success by how little time my students have to consult their laptops."

Harlene looked aghast at the very thought of such a notion. Ramble thought she might power down her laptop and flee the room.

Sean McCarty, who taught communication skills, jumped into the developing breech with one of the generic questions prepared earlier in the day by a subgroup of the hiring committee. Sean was serving on his first university committee. "What qualities would you bring to the mentoring of student groups at our campus?" Sean read from the question list, his voice betraying some nervousness.

"Do you mean would I help in mentoring African American students here?" Nadine asked.

"Well, I guess that's what this question implies." Sean ventured a tiny smile as he pointed to the list in front of him. Ramble assumed the young man had learned a valuable experiential lesson about generic interview questions.

"Yes, Ms. Watkins, we *would* like to see the person hired for the position take an active role in mentoring diverse student groups here at our college." Renée removed her reading glasses as if expecting a challenge.

"I find that aspect of the position troubling," Nadine said. "Studies conducted among African American faculty make it clear we are *overemployed* in most institutions when expected to formally and informally advise students, serve on college committees, and engage with the community at large."

"You would refuse these important faculty roles?" Renée looked around the committee table to measure the others' reaction.

"No, not at all. But I would not do so at the expense of my classroom teaching, and my research and writing. I would also expect service beyond that of other faculty members would be noted in considerations of tenure, promotion, and teaching load."

Ramble expected Nadine had crossed a line Renée and some others supporting the college's diversity initiative held quite firmly. Judging by the cramped set of Renée's jaw, Ramble knew he was right. He had begun to wonder if Renée and her committee held to a vision of diversity in hiring, curriculum, and teaching that might shortchange African Americans whose long-standing call for representation in higher education, in Ramble's mind, shouldn't be ignored. Sure, a diversity that led to a deeper understanding of the world's and the nation's different cultures was something higher education should embrace. Ramble liked that ideal. But could the new emphasis and language of diversity initiatives submarine what Ramble used to understand as actions designed to right historical inequities? Exactly how were people in the academic world defining affirmative action and diversity these days?

Sweatman sighed loud enough to attract everyone's attention. He held up a ballpoint pen, clicking it again and again in front of his eyes. "Is there anything else you'd like to share with us about why you find this position so *troubling*?"

Nadine waited to answer until Sweatman had to look in her direction. Ramble would have yanked him around by his goofy tie.

"I suppose as a seasoned professor, Dr. Sweatman, you appreciate the need for what I'd call a power base. Isn't that so? The political reality of African American faculty is that we are vulnerable to a number of pressures in an academic setting like this one. We are often part of an isolated program within the curriculum and don't have a ready-made power base with all the protections and possibilities others may enjoy. As an individual—an African American and a woman—I could use some sort of power base." Nadine leaned toward Sweatman, searching his eyes. "Wouldn't you agree?"

Sweatman dropped his pen and affected a look of amazement. Many around the table shifted in their chairs, uneasy with the developing confrontation. The sneer curling Sweatman's lip drew a faint, "Oh, my," from Harlene. She drew back in her chair, pulling the ends of her sweater, appliquéd with playful pink poodles, tight across her bosom. To Ramble's eyes, even the poodles looked alarmed.

"Excuse my interruption, but do you have any questions for us, Nadine?" Sam smiled in Sweatman's direction as if the two were best of friends.

"How would you describe your campus environment for the hiring and retention of African Americans?" Nadine asked.

"You meant a campus climate for faculty of color, did you not?" Renée worked up a sizable frown.

"No," Nadine said, "I did mean African American faculty in particular."

The committee members averted their eyes and many gave full attention to rearranging and studying the papers and documents before them. Ramble caught Renée in a furtive move to place a check mark next to Nadine's name on a master list of candidates.

"I hate to cut off discussion," Sam said. "But we have a meeting with Dean Swilling in 10 minutes, and I'd like to allow Nadine time for some final words."

"Nice timing." Sweatman muttered. Ramble knew the agent provocateur to his left was sorely disappointed a developing confrontation would be short-circuited.

"Let me say just a couple of things." Nadine smiled again at the committee members. In the final minutes of the interview, Nadine touched on several problems and pressures faced by African American faculty in new settings, including inadequate mentoring systems; geographic and social isolation; student racism in the classroom, especially in courses taught by women; and a difficult expectation for Black faculty to fit in with what she called "the dominant culture" on a campus. In Ramble's mind, Nadine's final words seemed mere topic sentences for more lengthy discussions. Committee members listened politely but asked no further questions.

When the interview ended, Renée and Sweatman left without a kind word for anyone. The others wasted no time in escaping to their offices with mumbled words of parting to the candidate. Sam and Nadine rushed off for the dean's interview.

Ramble sat in the empty conference room, paging through files assembled for the two remaining candidates for the African American studies position. Neither candidate came close to matching Nadine's qualifications. Her appointment should be a no-brainer, but Ramble assumed his opinion wouldn't be in the majority.

CHAPTER 9

Late Wednesday Evening

"My God, Ray. What's wrong?" Alicia Ramsey watched Ray Kent sprint down the hall toward her.

"Call 911, Alicia."

"You look like you've seen a ghost." Alicia ran a nervous hand through her hair.

"Worse than a ghost."

"Are you serious?"

"Something's trussed up on a table in the biology lab, and it ain't a frog."

"What?" Alicia grabbed at Ray's shirtsleeve, her brown eyes wide with alarm.

"Just call, Alicia. Quick."

Alicia fished a cell phone out of her jeans and punched 911.

Ray raced back to the biology lab. He didn't want anyone else to see the body on the table. High-pitched screams echoing down the hall told him he was too late. Two students blocked the doorway, books and purses piled about their feet, hands covering their eyes. Ray pulled them away from the opening. They hugged and blubbered, eyes wide, tears gushing.

Ray pleaded with the students. "I know it's a shock, but you need to stop."

Alicia hurried toward Ray, cell phone pressed to her ear. "The police are on their way. Can I look?"

"Come on, Alicia. Stay out here and wait for the cops." Ray pointed at the students, who now cowered near a hallway window. "See if you can calm those two down."

Inside the lab, Ray edged near the large wooden table where over the years thousands of Välkommen U biology students had sliced and diced frogs, fetal pigs, and possibly a few fingers. The man's body lay face up, clad only in a pair of boxer shorts emblazoned with Disney cartoon characters, hands and feet tied with nylon rope and head encased in a plastic waste bag used to dispose of fragmented frog bodies left over from students' attempts at dissection.

That's how he died. Ray lightly fingered the plastic bag covering the man's head. *Suffocated, the poor fool. But what's with the rest?* The body had something wedged into its belly button, partially obscured by a fleshy roll of fat. Ray leaned down for a closer examination.

"Is that what I think it is, Ray?" Alicia peered from behind Ray's shoulder at the object. "Yeeuuuh. That is *so* gross. It's . . . a tongue."

"Alicia. For cripes' sake. I told you to stay out." *But it was a tongue.* Ray leaned back and surveyed the body as Alicia clung to him, shivering. Her breath came in quick gulps. She rested her face against Ray's arm. The fresh smell of shampoo in her hair masked the sour tang emanating from the dead body on the table.

"Are you all right, Alicia? You'll make yourself sick." Ray's uncle owned the funeral parlor in Nagurski Creek, the small northern Minnesota town of his childhood. Ray and his cousins had seen many a dead body. Of course, the stiffs at Uncle Ralph's didn't have their tongues cut out and stuck in their belly buttons.

"This is why I quit med school." Alicia hugged Ray around his waist before retreating toward the door. As she went through the door, Ray could glimpse the two frightened students holding each other, somewhat calmed, snuffling, tears sopping their cheeks. Ray pulled a ballpoint pen from his pocket, carefully inserting it under the vagabond tongue, where someone had wedged a slip of paper.

"Are you kidding me?" Ray hadn't bargained for such a bizarre night on the job. All he wanted was a little extra cash, not *CSI*. He'd applied for one of the university's work-study positions, accepting a spot working nights for the biology department. From 8:00 p.m. to midnight, three days per week, he cleaned sinks and lab equipment. Before leaving, he had to lock everything down tight. The previous semester, students had taken advantage of lax security to filch a variety of specimens—fetal pigs and sheep's organs seemed most enticing to the thieves. In the equipment category, anatomical torso models topped the list of pilfered items.

Ray usually spent most of his four-hour shifts down at the computer lab, working on his course assignments and trying to romance Alicia. Tonight, at the start of his shift, Ray finished cleaning the biology lab in a half hour. He glanced at his watch. The cops would want to know what time he found the body. The digital display read 10:45 p.m. Whoever did this guy in had plenty of time to spare.

Ray tipped the tongue up once again to read the note. It was some sort of song lyric.

> *Go tell that long tongue liar*
> *Go and tell that midnight rider*
> *Tell the rambler, the gambler, the back biter*
> *Tell 'em that God's gonna cut 'em down.*

"Exactly what I wanted on my night off," Detective Jarvis grumbled. Pulled out of their beds, eyes puffy and clothes tousled, the two detectives looked like sleepy preschoolers. They stood at the victim's feet, the toes now turning a ghastly shade of purple. Phan plucked the elastic at the waist of the dead man's Disney underwear as he moved alongside the table. "Enough to make you a Mouseketeer."

"Whatever happened to tighty-whiteys?" Jarvis asked.

"It's all about personal expression." Phan leaned over the body for a closer look, pointing at the excised organ. "This'll set tongues wagging on campus."

Jarvis picked up the beat. "The brass downtown will give us a hell of a tongue-lashing if we don't solve these murders."

"Tell me what's going on here." Phan demanded.

Jarvis studied the bonds lashing the dead man to the wooden table. "I'm tongue-tied."

Phan pointed to the corpse's empty, gaping mouth. "No more irony and satire for this guy."

"What?"

"You know—tongue-in-cheek stuff."

Ray stood in the background watching the detectives, enjoying their routine.

"Hey, young man." Jarvis called over his shoulder. "Any theories about what's happened here?"

Ray didn't know what to say.

"Cat's got his tongue." Jarvis winked at Phan.

Ray thought for a few seconds. "No theory yet, but it's on the tip of my tongue."

"Enough! Take his statement." Jarvis feigned a tough-guy glare at Ray. "And, kid, you better not be speaking with a you-know-what."

CHAPTER 10

Two Weeks Later

Assistant Dean Billings paced in front of Ramble's office door, a look of pained administrative exigency puckering his face. Ramble knew that look. Billings was about to dump something on an unsuspecting faculty member, and that lucky fellow was none other than Jack Ramble.

"No, Abel, I can't help you." Ramble pushed his key into the door lock, shouldering the dean aside.

"No fooling you, eh?" Billings tried his most pleasant smile. Practice did not make perfect, Ramble concluded. The assistant dean's smile looked like a weasel with hemorrhoids. "I'm here to make you a good deal."

"Your good deals are a no deal in this professor's world."

"Indeed." Billings had raised his squeaky voice loud enough so any student or professor in the hallway could hear him. He kept the weasel smile plastered on his face. "We wouldn't ask unless it was absolutely crucial for our students, believe me. Dean Swilling and I need you to teach a late-afternoon honors course. Can't you find it in your heart to help out? I know the students will really appreciate the effort."

"You little runt." Ramble took a step forward and grabbed the assistant dean's arm, pressing into a nerve, maneuvering him to a nearby alcove. Billings struggled to extract a document from inside his blazer, snagging an expensive gold watchband on his red knit tie. Ramble snatched the document.

"It's an overload payment signed by the dean," Billings whispered, his eyes darting back and forth. "She's willing to pay you at an enhanced overload rate."

"So the dean will pay top dollar, and you're trying to hide the offer?" Ramble's voice boomed up and down the hallway.

"Just say you'll do it and sign the overload contract." Billings's eyes started to tear from the pressure Ramble held on his arm.

"I want a healthy book budget, an iTouch, courtside tickets for the Timberwolves, and your snazzy office chair." Ramble enjoyed watching the outraged reaction to his teasing.

Billings wriggled out of Ramble's grip and fled down the hall to the stairwell. He paused on the first step, straightening his tie and fluffing up his authority. "I'll let dean know you've agreed in principle. The class meets in thirty minutes."

Ramble nodded. It made sense to allow Billings a shred of dignity.

The department's seminar room held a sizable conference table of polished cherry wood—a gift from the Alumni Club. The fifteen swivel chairs surrounding the table fit that exact number of students who looked anxious as Ramble entered the room armed only with a yellow legal tablet, a ballpoint pen, and a couple of whiteboard markers. He dropped the items at the head of the table and made a comic about-face, hurrying back to the department offices to find another chair. He poured the last of the day's coffee in a paper cup, wishing that acquiring a theme and substance for the honors course could be as easy.

"Welcome to the honors seminar, scholars." Ramble numbered to fifteen on a sheet of the yellow tablet and turned to the first student on his left. "Let's go around the room so you can introduce yourself. Tell us your name, what year you are, and why you're in this class."

"I'm Ron Hightower, and I'm a sophomore." The student kept his eyes on the notebook in front of him, his fingers tapped lightly on the cover. "Sorry, but I'm really not prepared to give a good answer as to why I'm taking this honors course."

"An honest man." Ramble leaned forward, trying to get the student's attention. "I'll be honest too. I have no idea what we're going to study."

"Is that a good thing?"

"I certainly hope it will be, Mr. Hightower."

Ramble asked the student on Hightower's left, "How about you? Do you think we can make something out of nothing?"

"As sure as my name is Melody Petersen. I'm a junior, and I say why not?"

This might have the makings of a fun class, Ramble thought. He wrote down Melody's name. "How might we go about our task?"

Ramble watched the precocious Ms. Petersen fuss with a lock of auburn hair, sweeping it back behind her ear. She seemed to enjoy being front and center. "I suppose we could study just about any subject as long as it related to American literature. That's your field, isn't it?"

"Yes. I suppose it would be helpful sticking with what I know best. But let's not worry about me." Ramble nodded at the next student, a few years older than the rest with the unshaven look favored by Hollywood's popular leading men. He looked familiar. The student pointed to himself, somewhat unsure if he should continue the round of introductions. Ramble indicated he should.

"I'm Ray Kent. Let's see. Oh yeah, I guess I'm a sophomore."

"You're the one who found the body, aren't you?" Melody stared at Ray.

News and rumors about the latest murder continued to occupy everyone's thoughts across the campus. Melody was right. Ray had found Professor Briney Sweatman's body in the biology lab, and Ramble assumed the young man had spent many hours since then with the homicide cops.

"Any ideas for a theme, Ray?" Ramble asked. "Something that'll still qualify as an honors literature course?"

"I'll take a pass on this one for now. Thanks anyway, Professor."

"No problem." Ramble looked around the table for someone who might have an idea. No response. "OK. I'll shut up for a couple of minutes while you think about some angles for our course."

Ramble hoped one of the students would have at least an inkling of what the class might pursue. He thought about his own undergraduate days and how students cried out to study what made a difference in their lives and to the world around them. He could still recall the courses, readings, and projects connected to what most concerned and interested him during his college years. The compass of these few opportunities motivated him to learn, to work at a higher level, to appreciate his professors. Was he the exception? Were the students around the seminar table that different? Ramble didn't think a quantum lapse in human nature had transpired. Students liked to study what made a difference in their lives. Didn't they?

"Let's continue our introductions, and come on, let's hear what really grabs your interest these days."

"Professor Ramble?" Ray had his hand raised. "Excuse me for interrupting, but I guess I do have an idea. I don't know how it would fit, but what's been going on here these past few weeks hits pretty close to home for all of us. Is there something we could do with all that?" The student ran his fingers across a stubble of whiskers, looking around the table at the other students.

Ramble nodded at the suggestion but hoped the class wouldn't go in that direction. "I wonder if that would be quite the right thing?" It didn't seem so. Ramble waved at a freckled, smiling face from last semester's introductory survey course. "Hey, Josh. What do you think?" *Come on kid. Serve up a winner.*

"I was remembering that riff you gave last year on Edgar Allen Poe and the murder mystery story. I'm not sure, but I like those whodunits." Josh looked around the table to gauge the groups' reaction. Several of the students nodded in agreement.

"That would be way cool," someone at the other end of the seminar table blurted out.

"Outstanding," Melody echoed.

The enthusiasm for Josh's idea drained Ramble's hopes for an entirely different subject. "Shouldn't we weigh some alternatives?"

Ramble asked. Anything but the campus murders, especially when the local fuzz had his name on a list of possible suspects.

"Oh, man. Let's do it." Josh said.

"This'll be amazing. And you asked us for a topic," Melody said, conjuring up her most innocent face. "Besides, a bunch of us are in the creative writing course. This could be a great combination."

"See." Josh folded his hands on the table and grinned.

"This is going to require a lot of quick planning." Ramble's thinking out loud only served to fuel the students' enthusiasm for the road untraveled. They burst into conversation.

On the short drive to his small two-bedroom ranch home near Highland Park, Ramble thought about the honors seminar. The students liked their idea of putting the campus murders front and center, but they weren't quite as sure about how to translate their fascination with it all into academic study. At any rate, he'd sent them packing with plenty to do before the next meeting. Ramble had some serious thinking to do about the class as well.

A dark blue four-door sedan blocked Ramble's driveway. He figured not many citizens drove a Ford Crown Vic with dual side-mounted spotlights. The St. Paul police detectives had a few more questions.

CHAPTER 11

"Not a one of these inconsiderate clods sent me a reply."

Ramble's old friend Professor Leo DaVita waved a sheaf of letters in the air. He struggled out of a well-stuffed easy chair and limped toward his office window. He yanked up the blinds and gazed out at the bleak rain-spoiled morning.

"They're probably afraid you'd make them look bad, Leo."

"Don't hand me that bull."

A professor of history at age 68, now two years out of harness after his retirement, Leo hadn't mellowed from the experience as far as Ramble could tell. Leo gestured at the mess about his office—a cramped space with a jumble of mismatched rejected furniture, books and papers jammed in every nook and cranny, old classroom hanging maps, and boxes of research notes. "Damn it. You'd think this university would give a revered professor emeritus like me some updated accoutrements in this half-assed office."

"Leo. Relax. You're going to blow out a fibulator if you don't watch it."

Ramble was hiding out in Leo's fourth-floor office this day. Professor Sweatman's demise, what the students dubbed the "dice and slice caper," had put Ramble in an unwelcome spotlight. He'd spent more than a few hours answering questions lately, including the night before, and the detectives said they'd be back. If nothing else, the comedic constables, Jarvis and Phan, would be true to their word.

After his retirement, the university allowed Leo DaVita space in a converted janitor's supply room well out of sight and out of contact with his former department. The retired professor came in every day to work on what he claimed would be a "major, revisionist monograph on early nineteenth-century debtor laws." As Leo admitted to Ramble, "About five old fools like me in the country will read the damn thing, but someone's got to do it. The university presses need *something* of substance to publish." Finding obscure, useless, and absurd university press books amused Leo no end. Each week he sent Ramble an e-mail with another of his favorites. Last week's was titled *Optimality Theory: Surreal Flavors of Dairy Queen Blizzards and Critical Thinking as Constraint Satisfaction.* Leo swore the book was the first in a series.

"I have sent out my offer to teach a course, without compensation, to a total of fifteen local colleges and universities." Leo plopped down in his easy chair again. The light from the nearby lamp registered a swirl of dust from the ancient furniture. "But, I ask you, do I get any replies?"

By the time he retired, Leo had managed to piss off most of the administration, particularly Assistant Dean Billings. The dean made it clear to Ramble and others that hiring Leo for any sort of teaching, short of introductory night courses at a distant suburban site, would cost them dearly in one way or another. All Leo could count on from the administration was temporary office space, despite the fact he ranked as one of the most popular teachers in the school's history. He kept up on his subjects and would have liked to continue teaching an on-campus course or two. Ramble advised him the chances were slim to none he would have a chance to teach. So Leo sent out a letter of inquiry along with his substantial résumé to the chairs at several institutions in the Twin Cities region.

"Not only don't they want me to teach, but these so-called colleagues in the profession won't even write me back. What the hell is that all about? Whatever happened to professionalism?" Leo sailed one of his books across the small office space, crashing it into a pile of like objects cluttering a lower bookcase shelf. "Basic collegiality might suggest some sort of reply, don't you think? What a bunch of jerks. Why wouldn't they take advantage of my offer?"

"Do you expect most department chairs to practice the niceties of running a business?" Ramble also wondered if most department chairs ever gave much thought to recruiting first-rate adjunct faculty like Leo. Of course, something like that would require extra work. It might also be a threat to their department's professors. Most academics, in Ramble's estimation, feared even the slightest hint of competition, despite the fact their departments needed all the adjunct teachers they could lay their hands on.

"You don't need the hassle, Leo."

"It's not a hassle. For crap's sake, I've taught all my life, and I want to keep teaching a bit." Leo sighed, glaring at something across the room.

"Why not develop a hobby?"

"Teaching and research are good enough hobbies to keep me busy, don't you think? What do you want me to do? Take up stamp collecting? Collect American Girl dolls? Travel? I hate airports." Leo lifted an eyebrow at Ramble. "Just wait until you retire, my friend. You ought to be prepared for the indignities."

"I'm already thinking ahead, Leo." Ramble lied. His thoughts about retirement at the moment only included the things he wouldn't miss about faculty work. But what were the things he couldn't easily replace?

"Well, don't rush it." Leo pointed a shaky finger in Ramble's direction. "You think retirement will be great when you're planning on doing it. But you can make some big mistakes, and I don't mean just money sort of things."

Ramble did worry that once he retired the department might let many of his initiatives slide. He'd seen it happen before. A new chairperson, particularly someone recruited from outside the department, might walk in and drop what Ramble had labored years to put into operation. It would be difficult being on the sidelines, watching some of his most prized ideas displaced. Would the department members he'd backed and helped mentor find themselves without support? He'd hate to see that. What about all the work he and his secretary had done on marketing literature courses for the department? E-mails, a Web page, posters, and extra advising at registration had goosed up course enrollments over 20%. Worst of all, would the idiots he'd eased off important committees find a way back into power?

"Identity. That's what you need to preserve." Leo rolled out of his comfy chair once again to fiddle with the blinds. "You can't turn off being an intellectual. You can't take the academic life home in some sort of retirement kit."

"While you're over there grousing about your fate, see if the boys in blue are looking for me." Ramble hoped the detectives had better things to do than chase him down. But he recognized why the lawmen would want him under the spotlight. Briney Sweatman and Roland Norris had occupied the lowest rung on Ramble's ladder of faculty acquaintances at the university. He and Briney had crossed swords some years before.

The two had attended the same grad school. Their academic departments fielded intramural sports teams in flag football and basketball. Keen rivalries developed, spurred on by a few of the younger professors who organized and played on the teams. Ramble's advisor in the English department recruited Ramble to play, and he gained a highly skilled hard-nosed player who liked to win. In one of the basketball games, Ramble suffered a sprained ankle early in the second half. His absence allowed the political science team to close within a couple of baskets with only two minutes remaining. Then Ramble limped back into action to preserve the victory. He could still toss in a shot without jumping, and he fired one up from the corner. As he watched the ball plummet through the net, a player from the opposing team stepped hard on Ramble's bad ankle. He roared in pain at the guy who did it. Briney Sweatman's pleasure lasted as long as it took Ramble to deck him with a hard slap across the face.

"Ramble, are you listening to me?" Leo waved a hand at Ramble.

"Sorry, Leo."

"I've lost my identity . . . or at least the one I liked best." Leo pulled off his reading glasses and examined the lenses for dirt. "All of a sudden

I go from being a respected teacher, scholar, and university decision maker to some old cluck who roots around in the broom closet. I could be the janitor for all my department knows. My old students don't even know where I roost."

"That's hardly true, Leo." But Ramble knew many of the younger professors in the department had no idea about Leo's former status.

"I don't have anywhere to go to talk about things intellectual now," Leo said.

"I thought the janitor had an MA in cliometrics or something."

"He's a good janitor, nonetheless." Leo glared at the computer on his desk. "This machine hasn't worked right in two months. You think I could get one of the computer techs up here to take a look?"

"Tell them downstairs to put you on the mailing and repair lists." Ramble made a mental note to speak to someone about it.

"Oh, hell. Why bother." Leo played with a rip in the green corduroy fabric of his chair arm. "Did you know all my old pals in the department have retired and gone to Florida or some place like that? They wear silly Hawaiian shirts and talk about 'gap wedges.' We used to get together socially. I miss that. If I went to one of the department's holiday parties now, I wouldn't know anyone. And what would I have to talk about anyway?"

Ramble remained silent while Leo talked, sneaking a quick glance at his wristwatch. He didn't have any good ideas to help Leo out of his funk.

"I think one has to weigh the benefits of retiring as early as I did. It seemed like the time to go," Leo said. "Hell, all the American historians in the department are doing microsocial history and gender bending now."

"Gender bending, Leo?"

"Something like that. You know what I mean. I don't doubt their approaches are worthwhile, but I feel like a third wheel. Hasn't your field passed you by yet?"

"It's trying, I'm sure," Ramble said.

Leo pointed a finger at Ramble. "I may be out of the life, but don't get out of it before thinking about an exit to a real future."

"Do something with that thought, Leo." Ramble figured with the baby boomer retirements cresting, professors could use some sort of mentoring about the next phase of their lives. Many colleagues would need help weighing their alternatives. "Seriously, Leo, what could you do to help people avoid your depressed, decrepit, derelict fate?"

"OK, I know things aren't as bad as I make them. I like your suggestion, sort of." Leo traced circles with the mouse of his computer. "You know what I'd ask the graying, stumbling hoard of senior professors?"

"No, Leo."

"I'd ask if they owed anything to the academic community this late in their careers. Perhaps I'd ask them what capacities . . . what power do they have as senior faculty? What's worth a fight to change?" Leo placed both hands on the desk surface and lowered his reading glasses on the bridge of his nose. Ramble could see he wasn't finished with the subject. "I know a good one. What sort of rock-bottom, essential knowledge can the senior professor bequeath to younger colleagues? And how about this? When all is said and done, dear colleagues, what do you want your legacy to be?"

Ramble gathered up his briefcase and gym bag from the floor. "Here's another one for you, Leo. If you had a chance to give students a last lecture, what would it be?"

"I read about the professor who did that last lecture for his students." Leo prepared to leave his office, gathering up a worn leather briefcase and a St. Paul Saints vintage baseball cap. "What an interesting idea."

"You really ought to do some mentoring or tutoring with younger faculty. You might be good at it."

Leo eyed Ramble like he'd dropped a bucket of fish guts on the floor.

Later that evening, right in the middle of a terrific double-play rally ender by the Twins' infield against the Tigers, Ramble's doorbell jangled. He glanced through the front window and recognized Detectives Jarvis and Phan standing on the front porch again. Their insistent ringing and thwacks on the door left little doubt the detectives cared more about their murder investigation than twin killings at the Metrodome.

No matter what Ramble said to discourage them, the detectives kept prying. Somehow they'd pieced together enough about his military service in the Army's Special Operations forces in the early 1970s to fuel a new round of questioning. Ramble never spoke about it, and most of that career would remain off the books, buried deep in the Pentagon's archives. But the detectives thought they had something.

"Someone with your training could easily do some major harm." Detective Jarvis scratched behind the ears of Ramble's dog, Mr. Silly, a golden retriever-collie mix. Mr. Silly rested his head on the detective's knee and cast up his moonstruck eyes in complete submission. Ramble snapped his fingers at the dog. Mr. Silly scrunched up closer to the man caressing him.

"Yes, Detectives. Norris or Sweatman would have been an easy target." Ramble's voice betrayed his growing anger. "As you must realize, most of the senior citizen population of Minneapolis, St. Paul, and nearby suburbs could have done the same thing."

"Come on. Norris was a big man. You're exaggerating." Phan said.

Mr. Silly, always the thoughtful, sensitive canine, shifted his attention and bulk toward Detective Phan, sniffing the inside of the detective's pant leg. Ramble hid his grin. A wary Phan stared down at the dog.

"Look, Detectives. It's been a long day, and I'd like to help as much as I can," Ramble couldn't resist saying it, "but you're barking up the wrong tree."

"Really?" Jarvis smiled at Ramble. "Make no bones about it, Professor, we'll keep digging."

Mr. Silly left the gathering and padded into the kitchen.

"Come on, Professor, help us put some flesh on this bone." Phan edged forward in his chair. "Where were you the night of Professor Sweatman's murder between nine and midnight?"

"Sitting in my living room, reading."

"That's the best you can do?"

"Ask the dog."

Mr. Silly shuffled into the room on cue and dropped his saliva-coated stew bone on Phan's well-polished brogan.

Interview over. But given the look in the detectives' eyes, Ramble knew they had bones yet to pick.

CHAPTER 12

"What happened to you?"

Melody Petersen and the other students in the honors seminar looked at their professor with concern. Ramble had forgotten to shave that morning after a night of tossing and turning with little sleep. The students had been talking about the campus murders when he arrived in the classroom. Ramble hoped his role in the drama wouldn't become general campus gossip.

"I asked you to do some background work last session for today's class. What have you got?" Ramble plopped down his briefcase and a stack of handouts on the seminar table.

"I brought a list of classic murder mysteries." Josh pushed his bibliography across the table at Ramble. "I found some prof's syllabus for a mystery and literature course too."

"I've got some how-to books on mystery writing," Melody said.

The other students hauled out a miscellany of what they'd discovered working on the assignment. The seminar table quickly piled up with books, articles, reviews, and printouts from Internet sites. Some of the students had gone directly to the Internet to do their assignments, not to the university library or its cache of online subscription academic sites. Wikipedia predominated, and Ramble wondered if he should spend some quality time with his students teaching them how to vet the good from bad Internet sites when researching assignments. He knew the librarians had such a workshop for all entering students, but too often the students seemed not to have incorporated the instruction into their scholarly pursuits.

Ramble gathered up the students' materials and gave them a quick look. "Thanks for jumping into the assignment with such enthusiasm. Some of you might want to consult the librarians about making good choices for research information. They'd love to help. Maybe we can spend a session talking about research and literature."

Polite silence informed Ramble such a session wouldn't exactly thrill the group.

"I have some ideas about what we might do in the next couple of weeks." Ramble looked around the table at his students. "But what are you thinking?"

"Let's go digital." Dressed in a dark blue T-shirt and jeans, with dyed jet-black hair, a flawless complexion, and deep green eyes, a young woman seated farthest from Ramble made the suggestion.

"It's Patricia Heinke, isn't it?" Ramble asked.

"I go by 'Starry' if you don't mind."

"What is it you're suggesting? It sounds interesting."

"She's probably talking about setting up a wiki." Melody plucked at the front of the revealing navy blue top she wore, unwittingly raising the testosterone level among the guys in class. Ramble had yet to adapt a scholarly pose toward the plunging necklines and hip-hugging jeans favored by most of the young women on campus. He was mostly embarrassed.

Melody glanced over at Starry. "You're in Professor Teche's course, aren't you."

Starry returned a cold gaze, remaining silent.

"Forgive me. But I am really out of the loop on all this stuff." Ramble looked around the seminar table for help. "Digital? What are we talking about?"

"It's like she said," Starry replied, indicating Melody with the barest civility. Some of the other students nodded in agreement.

"A wiki?" Ramble asked. Wasn't that some character out of *Star Wars*? He hoped Angela might know something about all this crazy stuff.

"Yeah. That's the idea," Starry said.

"OK. I'll tell you what. I'll think about it before we meet again next week. Maybe we can give it a wing." Ramble paused to collect his thoughts. "Today, I thought I'd give you some background on the origins of the murder mystery in American literature."

"It's a lecture, then?" Starry pulled her legs under her and closed her notebook. A few students appeared to react to Ramble's suggestion with the same indifference.

"Well, it's not like I'm going to pull out a podium and drone at you."

Why wouldn't it make sense to give the students a good shot of what he knew about the topic? They had to start someplace. He doubted most came with a ready-made framework for study.

"I like your lectures, Professor Ramble." Darryl Rousch, an advisee, had been a student in Ramble's American literature courses. Darryl ignored the soft groan from some of his classmates. "I say we can't start on a road from nowhere. I'd like to hear what you think."

"Thanks for the vote of confidence, Darryl, but maybe we should take a straw poll." Had he underestimated the level of his students? After all, it was an honors' class. He should have taken some sort of first-day survey.

"We don't have to vote." Starry kept her head down, paging through one of the books she'd brought to class, a slight blush radiating across her cheeks. "What if we asked you some questions instead?"

"Oh, great idea." Melody murmured, rolling her eyes.

"Did you have something to add, Melody?" Ramble asked.

Melody gave Ramble a coy smile, stretching like a cat after a long nap. The guys went on full alert. "I'll vote for the lecture. As you said, it's not like you're going to deliver the Gettysburg Address." Ramble knew Melody intended her remark for Starry.

"Now that I think about it, I like Starry's suggestion." Ramble watched Melody's confidence slip a notch. "Fire away with your questions. I'll try to keep my answers compact."

After some forty minutes of questions and answers, and a couple of good exchanges between the students, the class had covered much of the background material Ramble intended to set forth. Their questions revealed to Ramble what his students knew. What they didn't ask gave him a good idea about the research the students needed to pursue for the next meeting. Ramble felt excited about his students' possibilities and what they might accomplish. Not a bad class, he thought. Ramble decided to drop by Angela's office. He'd found a good excuse to see her again.

"I hardly qualify as an expert on teaching and technology, but I don't know why anyone would use half the stuff we've got in the class-rooms." Ramble stirred some sugar into the coffee Angela provided from a cool one-cup coffee brewer. He liked the deep flavor.

"You're not alone." Angela futzed with a disobedient printer behind her desk.

She'd twisted her long hair up this day, and the soft line of her neck fascinated Ramble. No wonder the Japanese placed such a high erotic priority on that meeting place of silken hair and smooth skin. Ramble decided the nape of Angela's neck could compete with the best from Tokyo to Kyoto.

"So what should I do?" Ramble asked. "I promised the class I'd look into this digital thing."

Angela leaned over the printer, stretching on tiptoes, searching the back of the machine for a loose connection. Ramble abandoned for a moment the Japanese map of sensual attractions.

"Why don't you talk with someone working on our instructional technology grant?" Angela slapped the printer and muttered something at it. "I know they have some good people over there."

"Would that be the same user-friendly bunch who'll never give you the time of day when you need them to fix things? Those who treat you like a blooming idiot? Those who speak in strange tongues?"

"No. You're thinking about the wrong people." Angela slid back into her desk chair and tapped a couple of keys on her computer. "Phooey. It still won't print."

Ramble hoped she might check the cords and connections again. Angela read his thoughts and gave Ramble a disapproving look. "If you need to know something about setting up a class Web site, go over to the teaching and technology project in the computer building."

Ramble sipped his coffee, thinking to himself. Students didn't need more of what they had taken to the extreme. They needed to talk with people who liked to discuss important ideas. Talking, listening, reading, writing, reflecting—there was a good prescription for active, substantial learning. Students didn't need extra doses of—what was it? Facebook. They needed real books with covers and pages. Somewhere Ramble had read another good prescription: Make sure your students put in some hard work to develop the intellectual stamina and the ability to ask questions that don't lead to easy answers. He didn't think messing around with technology all the time could accomplish that.

"I bet you're one of those." Angela pointed a finger at his chest.

"One of what?"

"Macho guys who won't ask for directions."

"Damn straight. That's why some macho guy like me invented the GPS."

Angela sighed and went back to futzing with the printer. "Why don't you think about how teaching technologies might enhance your work with the students? Would they save time for class discussions?"

"Give me a hint."

"How often do you sacrifice discussion and problem solving in your classes to cover content?"

"Not much I can do about that, Angela. Usually, in most of my regular classes when the kids need to know some fundamental things about the subject we're studying, I lecture."

"Any way around that?"

"Not unless I find a textbook I can trust to cover what they need to know—the way I'd like them to know it." Ramble tried to keep a straight face. Angela wasn't buying.

"You found a way around a lecture today, didn't you?"

"Yeah, but . . . I didn't need some computer thing."

"Oh look, Stan," a voice sounded behind Ramble from the doorway to an adjoining room. "It's Professor Ramble. Our very own academic mastodon."

Professor Merega Raund and her partner in crime, Professor Stanley Robin, stepped into the office from the adjoining seminar room. This pair served as faculty liaisons to the Teaching Center. Ramble knew them better as overseers and protectors of faculty prerogatives when it came to Angela's planning and budget. Merega and Stanley had controlled the faculty association for more than a decade. Their tyranny accounted for abysmally low rates of attendance at meetings—something they could not care less about. "The less there is, the more for us," seemed to be their mantra.

"Primordial soup, anyone." Stanley smiled at Ramble.

"You're perfect for the next workshop Stanley and I have scheduled," Merega said, edging closer to Angela's desk, her eyes scanning its surface. She took special interest in a small stack of newly ordered books. A tall woman, somewhere in her late 40s, burdened by 20 extra pounds hanging mostly from her middle, upper arms, and under her chin, Merega spent a good deal of her academic waking hours championing the academic trends and fads—curricular, pedagogical, and managerial (Ramble and others still whispered "Management by Objectives" as she passed by). A Teaching Center workshop poster on the wall heralded her most recent fascination, Ego-Based Enhanced Learning. In turn, behind her back, faculty would softly sing a spin-off of Electric Light Orchestra's bygone top-forty recording "Evil Woman."

"Would it be of news to you, Ramble, that some very bright people in higher education, and excellent teachers as well, consider a lecture to be the ghost of a bygone era in academe?" Merega asked.

Angela sat on the corner of her desk, attempting to shield its surface from Merega's prying eyes, the toe of her black pump nudging Ramble's shin as a warning to stay cool.

"Sorry, Merega, but the 'guide on the side' is not my teaching thing," Ramble said, trying to further irritate the woman.

"Exactly, Ramble. I prefer to be 'the sage on the stage.'" Leo appeared in the doorway of Angela's office.

"Speaking of ancient species—" Merega dropped her armload of books on a table and returned to the seminar room with Stanley shadowing her every step.

"Don't knock it," Leo called after the retreating pair. "Experience matters."

Angela waved hello at Leo, squeezed past Ramble's chair, and offered the older man a generous hug. Leo looked over Angela's shoulder with a Cheshire grin. "What are we talking about here?" Leo prolonged the hug. "I'm sure I'll have an opinion."

"Merega thinks old fusspots like you who live and die by the lecture are standing in the way of authentic student learning." Ramble sensed Merega and Stanley creeping near the seminar doorway to overhear the conversation. This could be fun, he thought.

"Leo, I've learned there are highly effective ways to deliver content without a lecture," Ramble smiled at Angela. "But, with appropriate modification, lectures still have their place."

Settled in the chair, Leo glanced in the direction of the seminar room, raising his voice slightly to make sure Merega and Stanley could overhear. "I remain a staunch advocate of the traditional lecture approach for the college classroom. One-on-one intellectual healing and enhancement may have its place in some of the lesser disciplines, but not in mine."

"But, Leo, surely you'd admit that your students will do better with the latest active learning approaches. Wouldn't you?"

"Hogwash." Leo winked. "The real solution is better lecturing."

"But, dear colleague," Ramble gazed at the ceiling, as if pondering an important choice of words, "will great lectures help remake our students' maps of reality?"

Ramble could see Angela was uneasy with the teasing.

"According to what I've heard from your students, Ramble, you use a lot of class time for discussion and problem solving."

Ramble knew the time had come to stop baiting the pair in the seminar room. "Sorry, but I think we've gone too far—condemning the lecture and relying on all sorts of strategies and technology to do our jobs. Not every student walking into a classroom comes ready made with equal and elevated capacities for learning. Not to mention the motivation to do so."

"I agree." Leo said. "Our students are indeed a variegated lot, and in the traditional college age grouping, these youngsters come to us representing a significant array of personal, social, and cognitive stages of development. At least that's what the researchers tell us. But I ask, whatever happened to the thrill and benefit of observing a great mind at work? I dare say that listening to first-rate lecturers, the masters of their disciplines, not only motivates a student to attain the higher goals of the educated person but may provide admirable role models for upcoming adulthood."

"But how many great lecturers are there within one college?" Angela asked. "How do you provide a steady diet of great lectures for introductory courses in all the disciplines? What about the evidence that says very little of what is presented in the lecture, even a first-rate one, will stick in the students' minds as significant learning?"

"In answer to your last question, I'd say that's why we have assignments and exams for our students to apply their learning." Leo fingered the blue and gold striped tie he wore. "As to the other question you pose, I yield to your reasoning."

Ramble hated losing an opportunity to further irritate Merega and Stanley who had emerged from their listening posts and stood with arms crossed, glaring at him and Leo. He'd gone far enough, though, if the deepening frown on Angela's forehead meant anything.

"Seriously, Angela, I appreciate the value of having students learn in different ways and encourage them to do literary study. I have them doing a lot through my assignments and classroom exercises. But still—which of your undergraduate professors most influenced your intellectual development? Who got you excited about learning?" Ramble figured most would agree with his college experience. "For me, it was one of the great lecturers I had."

Angela turned back to joust with the computer printer.

"Personal charisma and lectures are antithetical to students' ego enhancement, self-paced learning, and intellectual self-discovery." Stanley Robin dutifully recited some of Merega's theories.

From what Ramble gathered in conversations with students, Merega and Stanley spent most of their energy drawing attention to themselves and increasing the students' dependency—something that could easily occur even in the classrooms of those whose pedagogical models emphasized guiding as opposed to telling. Whatever the approach to teaching and learning, Ramble thought, *who* was doing the teaching still made a difference.

"We'll leave you to properly educate these two, Angela." Merega nudged Stanley toward the doorway. "We're late for a meeting. The faculty association has selected us to serve on the librarians' materials acquisition task force."

Stanley laid a finger on the book package resting on Angela's desk. "We want to centralize acquisition systems."

Once the two professors disappeared through the door, Angela looked at Ramble and Leo as if they'd been sent to the principal's office for pulling pigtails. "Sometimes I'd like to wring both your necks," Angela said. "I won't have this job long if those two have their way."

"Don't worry about them," Ramble said.

Angela didn't look convinced.

Before leaving Ramble figured he'd better make amends. "Angela, where do I find the people you suggested in the Teaching With Technology Center?"

Angela opened a book package on her desk and surveyed the table of contents in one of the volumes. "Try your GPS, Studmuffin."

CHAPTER 13

Detective Jarvis stood next to Ramble on the steps of the computer sciences building. The bags under his eyes betrayed another late night investigating the campus murders. Detective Phan had the same burned-out look. Ramble had expected another interrogation, but he didn't have time today, what with a full afternoon of meetings and classes. "Can't you two guys find any credible suspects?"

Phan said, "You've got a history with both victims. What was it with you and Professor Sweatman?"

"Nothing to report, Detectives." Ramble stepped toward the library door. "Look, guys. Sorry I'm being a bit testy here, but I've got places to go and people to see."

"Hold on a second." Ramble could tell from the tone of his voice that Jarvis wasn't fooling around. "You and Sweatman didn't like each other. That right?"

"You wouldn't have liked him either."

"A witness reports you and the victim had a disagreement a couple of years ago," Phan read from his case notebook. "Care to tell us what that was all about?"

Ramble had never expected that particular episode would come back to haunt him. He'd stayed in his office late working on an article.

About midnight, on his way out of the building, scuffling sounds and voices drew his attention to the faculty lounge on the first floor. He found Sweatman with Dana Miller, a grad student working as an intern in the dean's office. How she'd ended up with Sweatman in the darkened room, Ramble didn't care to find out. She obviously didn't like whatever the pig had on his agenda. Ramble grabbed Sweatman by the scruff of his neck and shoved him into a cleaning closet, blocking any exit by tipping a chair up against the door handle. Dana didn't want to get involved and ran out of the building. She quit her internship the next day but not before calling Ramble to thank him for the rescue and asking him to keep the incident confidential. Sweatman spent part of the night with mops and a floor waxer. The building janitor on the early morning shift found him.

"I have the woman's name, and given the circumstances I'm sure she'd be willing to verify the facts," Ramble said, after outlining the incident for the detectives. "But I promised not to reveal her identity."

Jarvis rubbed the stubble on his cheeks, thinking. "We need her name."

"Let me ask her permission." Ramble didn't think Dana would object.

Jarvis sighed, "I'd really like to believe you, Professor."

"No problem. We can set up a Web site for your class on our network. I think these students can handle most of the design aspects." Alicia Ramsey seemed nice enough, and Ramble liked the way she explained Starry's "going digital" idea.

"I know Starry." Alicia tapped at her computer keyboard. "She hangs out here with a bunch of the other techies. They really understand a lot about programming."

"Do you think Starry's hanging around with the wrong group?"

Alicia frowned and looked toward the far corner of the room. "She could do better."

Beyond a row of sophisticated computer terminals, Ramble could see two students from his Introduction to Literature class, heads down, concentrating on their computer screens. Ramble watched Alicia fish among some brochures on her desk. She didn't look much older than most of his undergraduate students, but the young woman sitting next to him already had worked for one of the big educational publishing companies in their technology division.

"So what should I know about the modern world of technology and teaching?" Ramble asked. "What are some simple things I can do?" Ramble asked.

"I don't think it's really about using technology *for* teaching."

"Why so? It seems like everybody from the president down is pushing it and online programs." The rumors about several online degree programs the administration had in mind for the near future were probably true. The president's guru, Haney, spent an increasing amount of time "conferencing" with Dingkudgel about plans for the university's future.

"Oh. I don't mean distance learning technology," Alicia said. "I'm talking about the classroom. But I'm not recommending using technology for *any* teacher at *any* time. I think it depends on the class, the subject, and most of all, the specific goals for student learning in a course. You want the students involved and active with the subject and each other, not with the technology per se."

"I like that," Ramble said.

"If I understand correctly, you've got students who know their way around technology," Alicia said, "and they're excited about working it into a class project."

"You mean this learning object idea?"

"Yes." Alicia called up a couple of Internet sites on her computer screen from college courses around the country in history and economics. One of them was an extensive comparative collection of historical resources about the Civil War. She paused and smiled at Ramble. "What better thing could a teacher want than a class of students who have ideas and are all keyed up about following their noses?"

"OK, sure. But it depends if their noses are pointing in the right direction, doesn't it?"

"That's where your expertise comes into play. The other thing I like is the notion that technology can save class time for the most important activities."

"How do you mean?"

Alicia pushed away from her computer and faced Ramble. "Someone I know is in your class. It's only fifteen students, and he says they're all really bright."

"That's true."

"My friend says he and the other students like the interaction in the class and the face-to-face with someone as smart as you." Alicia gave Ramble an impish grin. "Of course, that last part is only hearsay evidence."

"Fair enough." Ramble saw Norman Cady enter the room, heading for one of the computers. He glanced at Ramble and Alicia before sitting at one of the computer tables, smirking about something.

"So if my friend is right," Alicia stole a glance in Cady's direction, "you want to save as much in-class time as possible for student-to-student and teacher-student interaction."

"Correct."

"So use technology to save time, to prepare your students, and to keep them thinking outside class." Alicia studied Ramble's face. "See the possibilities?"

Ramble could follow the argument but didn't know what the technological path would be. He guessed if his students used technology, along with the traditional sources of information about a subject—outside the classroom—it would open up a situation inside the classroom he and the students liked best for teaching and learning at a higher level. It was an honors class after all.

"So, Alicia. How do I go about engaging the technology to match your theory?" Ramble had no doubt the young woman had some answers at the ready. Within the next 25 minutes, he had things like course Web sites, course management systems, videoconferencing, podcasting, and several other possibilities rattling around in his head. He even had ideas for the class's desire to construct a learning object.

"And no PowerPoint?" Ramble liked the omission.

Alicia shook her head. "Some people use it very effectively."

"But it doesn't fit my teaching and learning goals?"

"Right."

"Praise be."

As Ramble left, Alicia called after him. "Welcome to the 21st century, Professor Ramble."

Ramble wasn't so sure. At least some of the things he'd learned about teaching along the way still counted. That was good.

Assistant Dean Abel Billings punctured Ramble's positive mood. The insufferable little bureaucrat was waiting for him in the hall near the main entrance to the English department. Actually, he waited behind an old metal desk in the hall, soon to be carted away by the janitorial staff. At the dean's shoulder stood the burly figure of Danny Elston, campus chief of security. Billings seemed unusually happy as he watched Ramble's approach. He had something up his sleeve no doubt.

"I'm so sorry to be the bearer of bad tidings, Professor Ramble."

"I'll bet."

"The unfortunate incidents on campus have taken a bad turn." Billings couldn't suppress a grin. "Until the official police investigation clears you of all suspicion, we have decided to suspend you from teaching."

Ramble didn't know what to say. The blood pounded in his head.

"Of course, Dean Swilling and I are convinced there is nothing to the rumors, although it gives us pause after hearing what the detectives have said about the investigation." Billings's smile morphed into a vile smirk. "We are caught between our desire to let justice run its course and our concerns about student safety on campus and in our classrooms."

Ramble stepped in Billings's direction. The administrator seemed to sense trouble brewing and edged toward the security guard. "Sergeant Elston will accompany you to your office. You can box up anything you'll need while we must deny you access to campus."

"Who's going to teach my classes? You, Abel?" It wasn't easy, but Ramble had recovered somewhat from his angry desire to ratchet the dean's head off his shoulders.

The assistant dean backed down the hall. "I'm sure we can find someone appropriate."

"You'd better." Ramble followed the dean's retreat. "The students shouldn't have to pay for your idiocy."

CHAPTER 14

He didn't want to die. For gosh sakes . . . his career was on a fast track.

After the dustup with Ramble in the hallway, Abel Billings retreated to his office, and behind a locked door, gave himself to the caress of his special-order "manager's choice," ergonomically correct, super-plush, cream leather office chair. Trembling hands and fingertips joined at his chest. He sought the inner peace guaranteed by his yoga relaxation tapes.

Drat. Calmness and inner peace eluded him. He shivered. That awful Ramble fellow could put a scare in anyone.

Abel flicked on the built-in body massager and tuned his chair's music system to a compact disk he'd purchased locally, *Pleasures Through Open Windows at Nightfall: Serenity Sounds from Reiko-San's Hennepin Avenue Spa.* He dialed down the office lights to a whisper with his automatic dimmer adjustment and burrowed further into the soft, comforting folds of his big chair, eyes shut tight, the massager cooing in his ears. That's when it happened. No warning. All he felt was a hand clap across his mouth and intense pressure on a nerve running up his neck.

When the blankness lifted, Abel's head felt awful. *I need to brush my teeth.* His tongue felt like it had been wiped with a wool sweat sock.

Wait a minute . . . What time is it? I can't move. Good grief! I'm not dreaming. I'm . . . gagged and bound.

Abel lay on the floor, his hands tied with his best red and black power tie, his feet fettered with the new cordovan belt he'd bought at the Future Deans Leadership Conference in Toledo. A wide slash of tape stretched across his mouth. On his chest, stacked like a mammoth order of pancakes, sat all the hardcover texts Abel had ordered (to sell at a later date) as exam copies from publishers.

The pressure on his chest felt like a vise. He could hardly squeeze the slightest breath into his aching lungs. The titles blurred on the hefty textbooks that rose toward the ceiling. *Were those the physics textbooks he'd just ordered, posing as the late Alan Spinkmeier, emeritus professor?*

The dark figure reclining in Abel's fancy chair listened at low volume to a discordant piece of modern classical music. The intruder reached to a shelf filled with impressive texts on higher education management, placed strategically so that anyone visiting with the assistant dean could see the titles in plain view.

"You pompous little creep. You've never read one of these books, have you?"

Abel could only manage a pleading look. He had read the chapter "Spend it Down: End of the Year Academic Financial Management," in Dr. Milly Frekmen's tome, *The Personal Economics of Academic Administration.*

"Here's one. *The Authentic Dean: Twenty-Five Administrators Speak Their Minds.*

Abel remembered that one too. He'd trolled through the table of contents but didn't recognize any of the contributors. All had retired many years before.

"Ooooo. Is it heavy?" The intruder placed the volume on top of the others already piled on Abel's chest and pressed down on the books with great force.

Abel's chest compressed and a rib snapped. He squeezed in a last fragile breath of air.

CHAPTER 15

"*Phew*. Your lawn positively reeks of media, Ramble."

Sam Agee and Angela stood on the front porch. Close behind the pair, a flotilla of microphones bobbed and weaved, the insignia plates of the various local channels clanking against each other in a crowded, pitched battle of the airwaves.

Ramble wished the ridiculous hacks would pack up and leave him be. For several hours, legions of brushed, lacquered, sprayed, tucked, tweaked, prompted, and spotlighted shills of sensationalism had prowled the lawn and curb outside Ramble's house. Their boneheaded live reports on the 10:00 p.m. news kept the neighborhood aglow with camera lighting despite a growing number of protests and catcalls by the residents. At least Ramble's longtime volunteer baseball coaching for the neighborhood kids had earned him a strong measure of support among parents. After a time, the intrepid members of the Fourth Estate, an appellation not one of the reporters outside could have explained, got the hint and stopped chasing Ramble's next-door neighbors for on-camera reactions to his predicament. Ramble particularly enjoyed the non-sound-bite response he'd overheard through his open window in answer to the Channel 9 reporter's predictable, numb-brained, "How do you feel?" question. Ramble's eighty-three-year-old neighbor, Mrs. Edna Hopkins, supplied a rambling, comprehensive answer. The young reporter obviously didn't have aging parents and relatives.

"You two are brave souls. Aren't you afraid of soiling your reputations?" Ramble glanced over Sam's shoulder at the turmoil on his front walk.

"Isn't this the Tupperware party?" Sam tossed his jacket on a chair in the living room.

Angela sat on the edge of the sofa, busy scratching a delighted Mr. Silly's ears. "How could they suspect someone who has such a sweet pooch?"

Mr. Silly thumped to the carpet and rolled over on his back, his front paws batting the air, delighted with the attention. With due regard to the dog, garrisoned inside his small one-story rambler, Ramble had sorely missed the companionship of his friends at the university. Stir crazy? It only took a few hours for that to happen. In that short time he'd been scheming how to break out of the jail imposed on him by the university and the media.

"Don't worry, Ramble. You have a lot of people on your side." Angela sat back, leaving Mr. Silly to loll in passion on the floor.

"I don't want to get mushy here, but even your students have rallied boldly to your cause." Sam sat down heavily on the old stuffed chair the dog often used when Ramble left the house. Mr. Silly hairs puffed up from the cushion and drifted about the chair. "But enough of feeding your ego. We have other things to talk about."

"What's up?" Ramble asked.

Sam knitted his fingers together in front of his chest, accompanied by a sigh. "You remember Nadine Watkins, don't you? The candidate for the African American studies position?"

"Hell, yes. I thought you'd offered her the job and she accepted."

"She did. But one of the committee members, Ken Flora, who we know doesn't like our candidate, launched himself into cyberspace for a night of Internet sleuthing. And citing such reliable sources as rankyourprofessor.com, MySpace, and YouTube, Dr. Flora has raised the issue of classroom bias."

"Yesterday, Ken called up a friend in California," Angela said. "It seems Nadine has run afoul of David Ternbot and his Students for Intellectual Diversity."

"What on God's green earth is that?"

"Don't you read the news, Ramble?" Sam pointed to the *St. Paul Pioneer Press* on the table next to him. "Ternbot is that sixties radical flip-flopper. He's convinced higher education is overrun with two-faced bleeding hearts, ex-revolutionaries, feminists, and—batten the hatches—snotty liberals. He's induced the SUV-driving, born-three-times-over, flag-humping, I'll-shoot-your-ass-off local state legislative types to sponsor bills protecting intellectually defenseless students from left-of-center political bias in the classroom."

"Whew. That must keep him busy." Angela touched her heart.

"So how, exactly, out of all the available academic left-wing liberal conspirators did Nadine get on this guy's list?"

Ramble vaguely recalled a proposal to regulate classroom bias intro-duced by Briney Sweatman similar to what Sam described coming from Ternbot's organization. Sweatman had presented his version in a way designed to sidestep any hallowed beliefs about academic freedom and freedom of speech. But Ramble understood the bottom line. Sweatman wanted his biases to get equal time, hoped to discredit any-one who didn't agree with his side of the political fence, and sought more recruits to the faculty ranks who shared his particular slant on the world. Ramble thought the whole *fairness* thing would dampen any discussion of contemporary issues in the classroom, no matter how relevant to a subject, how carefully and fairly presented, or how useful for students to consider in light of their unquestioned suppositions and myths. Follow the fairness prescription, and much excitement and passion would be lost from the classroom. Perhaps this Ternbot wasn't in the same duplicitous league as Sweatman had been, but Ramble wondered how the heck a campus could set up a formal structure and monitoring system to regulate fairness and balance? Besides, where was the proof that so many faculty members deliberately excluded views other than their own?

Ramble wondered if Ternbot and his followers were equally critical of the unspoken consensus held sacrosanct by a vast majority of profes-sors and academic disciplines about American exceptionalism, the fairy-tale version of free market capitalism, and two-party democracy? Most of what Ramble could identify as liberal in politics held fast to the basic fundamentals of American life. A liberal conspiracy in academe merely enforced the mainstream. In Ramble's experience, true progressive politics rarely found a voice on campus and among most of the faculty. Liberals and conservatives alike felt uncomfortable with progressives. So what's to worry, Mr. Ternbot?

"Nadine made a mistake." Sam's dark blue sweater now held several clumps of Mr. Silly's fur. "She invited a guest speaker to lecture in her course on the civil rights movement. He was with the Student Nonviolent Coordinating Committee in the early years. Apparently Nadine's guest had some pretty powerful, emotional stories about the civil rights murders in Mississippi. One of the students took some video on a cell phone of Nadine's reaction and the classroom discussion."

"The class turned very emotional," Angela continued the story. "Several of the kids were in tears."

"And that's what one student put on YouTube," Sam said. "Ternbot's Web site is showing it, and a couple of kids have written summaries of the class session for the *Student Exploitation Chronicle*. They accuse Nadine of messing with their heads about the civil rights movement and being too radical. She didn't invite anyone into class to balance the guest speakers."

"Who's she supposed to invite? George Wallace and the Knights of the White Camellia?" Ramble looked from Sam to Angela in disbelief. "Are we supposed to set up truth squads to roam from class to class?"

But Ramble did understand the type of students who might raise a fuss. Those on the far left side of the political continuum had always been a minority. Most college students mirrored the general, deep-rooted conservatism of most Americans. He expected that too many young men and women, despite their fascination with each other, popular culture, and technological gimmicks, had their eyes on little else but a high-paying career. Like most Americans in Ramble's view, students adopted the close-minded us-against-them worldview of their parents. No one really much talked about issues with an open mind anymore, with any shred of respect for another's viewpoint. Yell down anyone with a different take on an issue. That's how the penny-ante experts did it on TV. Ramble doubted late-night bull sessions—impassioned, but respectful talks about right and wrong, the meaning of life, and the betterment of humankind—had survived from his college days. *Hmmm. What a curmudgeon he'd become. Come on, now. Was he badly misreading things through his aging vision?*

He did know many students admitted to resenting course work that didn't seem to have anything to do with building a future career. That sort of thinking among students had been around for decades. But now, when placed in required humanities courses and the like, many students proved willing recruits or at least gave benign support to the appeals of a Sweatman or a Ternbot when asked to consider something outside their marketplace vision.

"It gets worse." Angela said. "There's some video of another class Nadine teaches, African American Political Thought."

Sam groaned, looking at the ceiling. "It's a bad moment, that's for sure."

"Sam's right. I saw the video," Angela said.

Ramble retrieved his laptop from the kitchen table and set it on the coffee table in front of Angela.

"Pretty soon, we'll have to make students check their electronics at the door," Sam said. "Just like the Wild West."

Angela downloaded the video from YouTube. The blurred, jerky segment shot from the back rows of Nadine's classroom showed her teaching a class of some 30 students. A student near whoever had the cell phone going asked Nadine, "Are we supposed to believe Nat Turner is some sort of hero?"

Nadine replies, "What are you trying to do here, Mr. Maas? You've asked the same question in several different ways so many times. We've spent quite a bit of time answering those questions."

The cell phone camera catches an African American student as she turns around to confront the speaker. "You think the slaveholders didn't use violence? Why should an oppressed slave be any different?"

"He killed one White woman," adds another voice in the background.

"That makes his use of violence OK?" asks the original questioner. "He should be a hero? Isn't that a great idea."

The camera shifts quickly to catch Nadine's reaction. She frowns and slaps her hand on the lectern. "Come on, Mr. Maas. I've said all along that the Turner story is very complicated and doesn't admit to any easy answers."

The student smiles like a choirboy. "So what's your bottom line?"

Several members of the class groaned and shifted in their seats, obviously uncomfortable with the situation.

"How many times do we have to revisit this?" Nadine's voice is strained. She looks at her watch. The class bell is heard in the background. "I suppose if you were in Nat Turner's shoes, Mr. Maas, you'd have brought in a conflict management team."

The students laugh. Nadine glares at the class. She squares her shoulders. "Would I use collective violence against oppression? Yes, probably I would. Try to use some historical imagination—" The shifting and clanking of desks drown out the rest of Nadine's response as the students rush to exit the classroom.

Ramble asked Angela to scroll back to the beginning of the download. He watched the class session another time. "It looks like she's very tired and frustrated."

"She's angry." Sam points at the computer screen, now frozen on Nadine's image at the front of the class. "Nadine's been having trouble with this particular group of students."

"She's defensive," Angela said. "And reacting to a student the way she did? Not good."

Ramble wanted more context for the incident. What else was Nadine saying at the end of the class when the bell rang? "On the surface, it looks bad."

"I've got a call into Nadine to get more of the story." Sam said. "It's a tough business if Renée uses this tape against Nadine's appointment. Plus there are several negative comments on those rate-your-professor Web sites."

Angela switched off Ramble's computer. "There ought to be some protections for faculty against videotaping without permission."

Ramble shrugged his shoulders. He couldn't recall any student in his classes taping him. He'd yet to look up his profile on ratemyprofessors.com. Maybe he should. "Someone who didn't hear all the discussion might certainly say she's advocating, pushing a certain political or moral position on her students," Ramble said.

Sam glared at Ramble. "She ought to be able to say and do what she thinks is best in her classroom."

"Hold on, Sam. I'm just speculating. I think it's a tricky line between encouraging controversy and, well, indoctrination."

"So you're saying *my* classroom isn't the place for me to urge students to some sort of action for good causes?" Mr. Silly edged away from Sam to the corner of the room, his ears back. "Don't I have the protection of academic freedom?"

"I think academic freedom is a tricky concept most of us fail to connect to real-world events," Ramble said. "We prattle on about it, but how many of us could give a good definition? I can't, and I guess I should be thinking more seriously about a working definition. How often do we really discuss it? With some exceptions, outside the classroom I guess we can shout our lungs out about what we believe and advocate what we'd like to see happen in the world, just as any *individual* American citizen should be able to do. That's freedom of speech. But I don't think academic freedom allows us the same latitude. I think it's about rights and responsibilities we have as professors, not individuals. It's contextual. It's called *academic* freedom for a reason." Ramble frowned. "But whatever it is, we sure as hell shouldn't be teaching to indoctrinate students."

"Do you care to define things like indoctrination and balance?" Sam asked. He rubbed his forehead. "Here's another question. How far does my classroom extend?"

"Exactly," Angela jumped into the conversation. "Does all this business apply to what a professor or an advisor does elsewhere on campus, outside the classroom?"

"Sorry, Angela. I admit to not thinking that far." Ramble headed for the kitchen.

Angela reached over the sofa back and caught the back of Ramble's belt. "Come back here, you. We're not through. I'm still worrying about Nadine."

Ramble allowed himself to be turned back to the sofa. "I don't think Nadine did herself any favors in the way she handled things. But over a whole teaching career . . . all those classes . . . how many of us haven't made mistakes or slipped up?"

Sam retrieved his coat and struggled into it. "What's our best shot then? I don't want to lose a chance to get Nadine on our faculty. How do I go about defending her candidacy?" He zipped up his jacket, pausing with his hand on the doorknob. "I guess part of it is deciding what the classroom represents and how teachers and students fit into that box."

Angela made no move to leave. "We need to think more about what it means to be a responsible teacher within the context of controversial ideas and opinions."

"I agree," Ramble said. "I'd like to have more to stand on than what we have right now, though." He didn't think things would end well. It seemed like one of those ambiguous situations he always warned his students about. No easy answers. Would the faculty committee ever come together for a useful discussion aimed at a reasonable solution about Nadine? Would they be willing to nail down a good definition of academic freedom?

"At the least, we should find out how to take advantage of good opportunities for learning when we're faced with these classroom controversies," Sam said.

As Sam walked to the door, Angela asked Ramble to give her a ride home later. "The media will be gone, and it'll get you out of the house."

Ramble did up some popcorn—one of his few culinary accomplishments. Angela located some bottles of Belgian beer. She also found a number of truly depressing items in Ramble's refrigerator. The three-week-old celery looked especially forlorn.

"You are invited to dinner this weekend." Angela passed an ancient plastic bag of coleslaw under Ramble's nose. It had a festering look to it. Mr. Silly sniffed the air optimistically, eyes bright with anticipation.

Ramble and Angela settled down on the living room sofa with the bowl of popcorn and beers. The dog sat close to Angela's legs and laid his head on her knee, moaning softly, watching her intently, pretend-ing no interest in the popcorn. Ramble thought maybe the mutt wasn't so silly after all.

Angela scanned some Web sites on the computer. She moved it over on the coffee table so Ramble could take a look. "It's a link from Tern-bot's Web site for student complaints. I guess they fill out a form, and then it gets listed here."

As they looked through the complaints, Ramble kept a mental tally. Most of the students filing complaints attended backwater universities and colleges—geographical directional schools of the academic uni-verse seemed to predominate on the listing. One confused complainant identified herself as a student at "Liberal Arts University." Another aggrieved party found a professor's habit of posting articles on his office door lauding his alma mater's successful football season deeply offen-sive. Articles extolling the student's home team apparently wouldn't have raised a hackle.

Ramble had to admit most of the complaints seemed to carry legiti-mate accounts. Professors were accused of mocking political and reli-gious figures, tearing down students' viewpoints on controversial events and issues, harping on things far afield of the subjects they taught, being needlessly offensive in their choice of classroom language and examples, and—attempting to indoctrinate.

"It looks like there's a fair share of half-baked professors who can make some truly outrageous out-of-context remarks." Angela shut down the computer and sat back on the sofa, shifting closer to Ramble. He could smell a warm scent of orange and ginger.

Mr. Silly now placed one paw gently on Angela's knee, signaling his affection. In a slow ballet of canine stealth, he crawled up next to her on the sofa. With a deep, shivering intake of breath, eyes still intent on Angela, Mr. Silly snuggled into the cushions next to his latest conquest.

"He is such a cutie." Angela winked at Ramble, her slender fingers ruffling through Mr. Silly's fur.

CHAPTER 16

Ramble turned into a maze of winding streets bordering the east side of campus. On the way home from Angela's, he'd received a surprise call from Starry, the young woman in his honors class. Her voice sounded small and hesitant—very much afraid of something.

"I'm really not sure, but I think there's something you ought to know. Can you meet me?" A long burst of static from Starry's cell phone covered her next few words. It sounded to him like, "at the back of the humanities building."

"Starry, wait. What's this all about?" No answer.

A For Sale sign in front of a darkened tree-lined driveway caught his eye. Ramble circled the block. Halfway back from the driveway entrance, he flicked off the car's headlights. He turned up the driveway, parking near a set of garage doors some 30 yards from the street. The owners, acquaintances of Ramble's, trusting that their real estate agent would come through for them, had cleared out and headed for Arizona to pursue a well-deserved retirement.

Moving across the Välkommen U baseball practice diamond, hugging the shadows, Ramble made it to the athletic building, avoiding the security checkpoint at the back entrance to the campus. A light glowed in the booth. Ramble could make out the security guard, slumped over a desktop, head resting on his arms. Around the corner of the athletic building and across a walkway at the north end of the quadrangle mall stood Gadda Administrative Hall. To the south, Ramble's office building rose four stories in a pale imitation of Ivy League architecture. Streetlamps cast dim pools of light on walkways bordering the quad. Ramble walked behind the buildings where only an occasional security spotlight stared out on empty service entrances. He reached the back door of the humanities building and waited, pressing into the shadows behind a lonely classical Greek sculpture banished years before from the main quadrangle. If he recalled correctly, the statue copied the famous Zeus of Artemision from the Archaic period, circa 450 BC. Through the bronzed legs, Ramble scanned the immediate area, his field of vision only partially impaired.

He detected movement, a small figure edging along the building wall to his right. Ramble drew Starry into the shadow where he stood. "What's going on?"

She put a finger to her lips, and pointed to the second-story administrative offices where thin red shafts of light flashed and danced inside a row of windows.

"It's Norman Cady and some of those kids."

"And?"

"Just go see what they're doing."

"OK. Stay here. I'll have a look."

Starry's eyes widened. She shook her head. "I'm too scared."

"Why? It'll be safer here."

"No. Please."

"Stay behind me then, and no noise."

Cady and his gang had already jimmied the main door lock. Ramble pushed open one of the double doors an inch at a time. Once in the building, Ramble and Starry moved along the side of a stairway leading to the second floor. At the top of the stairs, the red shafts of light dashed back and forth, crossing each other at crazy angles, blinking on and off in a confused sequence.

"They're having a laser fight." Starry clung to Ramble's arm.

Was this what Starry wanted him to see? A bunch of kids' games? Ramble knelt low and edged into the hallway, moving behind an abandoned janitor's wagon. From his hiding place, he could see a dark figure some 20 feet in front of him leaning out the doorway to the administrative offices, firing a laser gun toward another stairway down the hallway. Answering flashes came from at least three enemies in the game.

Ramble covered the distance to the doorway with large strides, the rubber soles of his running shoes muffling any noise. He knocked the laser gun out of the shooter's hands. It zigzagged down the hallway.

Ramble grabbed a head of greasy hair. "What the hell are you doing up here?"

The shooter made an angry sound deep in his chest. He slammed a fist into Ramble's ribs, and tried to follow with a kick. Ramble blocked the kick and grabbed hold of an ankle, jerking it skyward. The shooter fell back hard against the doorjamb. Stunned, the shooter slumped forward, falling slowly to his knees, pitching face first to the floor. Blood trickled from his nose.

Three pinpoints of red jittered on Ramble's chest.

"Cut the crap, you idiots," he yelled down the hallway. The laser beams disappeared, and Ramble could hear the pounding of footsteps down the back stairs. He ran the length of the hall following the retreating sounds.

"Hold it right there." An authoritative voice sounded at the bottom of the stairs, directing the fleeing culprits to stop. "Hands on the wall."

Ramble retraced his steps to find Starry gazing down at the body slumped unconscious on the floor. "It's Norman."

As Ramble and Starry eyed the body on the floor, at the far end of the building a dark figure eased through a seldom-used delivery entrance door and hurried into the shadows.

Detective Jarvis sat in a wingback chair facing Ramble and Starry in the reception area of the offices of the College of Liberal Arts. Detective Phan paced behind the sofa where he'd ordered Ramble and Starry to sit.

A woozy Norman Cady, his blood-caked nose relocated to one side of his face, waited in a far corner of the room guarded by a uniformed police officer. After a visit to the emergency room, Norman and his Star Wars compatriots would be driven to police headquarters in downtown St. Paul. On his way out the door, the punk gave Starry his best imitation of some street tough.

"Take care of that nose." Ramble smiled and gave a half wave in Norman's direction. The policeman pushed Cady out the door. Starry's lip trembled, but she fought back the tears. A few jerky breaths, a quick pass across her eyes with the back of her hand, and she seemed ready to answer questions from the detectives.

"What's this all about, young lady?" Phan's question earned him a critical frown from Jarvis.

Starry allowed one last tear to balance on her eyelid. "A couple of days ago, I sneaked a peek at the next segment of Norman's digital game design. It's like a Second Life 3D world. He's an ace at programming. We've been playing it and doing some virtual reality stuff with our characters. I got scared, though. I thought it was all just for fun . . . a game."

"I'm not getting the point," Phan said. "What are you and Professor Ramble doing here tonight? He's not supposed to be on campus."

"Phan. Let the girl explain." Jarvis waved a hand at his partner, motioning him to sit down.

"I found a way into a secret room in Norman's game. It turned out to be a game within a game." After a couple of deep breaths, Starry continued, "The new game . . . it was all about our school. The game was to plot against professors we didn't like. You know . . . kill some of the professors. I was worried they might be up to something awful tonight. I didn't know what to do, except call Professor Ramble."

"Which professors were targeted in the game?" Phan asked.

"There weren't any names."

A crash sounded inside the office behind Jarvis.

The detective moved quickly out of his chair, pivoting to face the office door. From inside his coat, he drew out an ugly-looking, jet-black revolver. He moved to one side of the office door, the top half of which held a beveled smoked-glass plate, emblazoned in bold script with the occupant's name and title: Dr. Abel Billings, PhD, Assistant Dean.

Positioning Ramble and Starry outside the line of fire, Jarvis raised his foot and kicked open the door. He and Phan dodged into Billings's office, their shoes crunching broken shards of glass. Standing at the office desk amid a scatter of books on the carpet, the detectives eyed the body in front of them.

"That's one for the books," Phan said, bending over to retrieve a heavy physics text from the floor.

CHAPTER 17

After speaking with Detectives Jarvis and Phan the day following the discovery of Abel Billings's murder, Ramble doubted enough evidence existed to make a murder case against Norman Cady. The little slimeball said he was just kidding around with the computer game, and the other students caught at the scene that night backed up Cady's protestations of innocence and supplied convincing alibis. The case remained open, but with the help of a hotshot public defender, Cady was released from custody. None of that put a stop to speculation led by a small coterie of faculty experts. Letters to the editor, guest editorials, televised interviews, calls to talk shows, mass e-mails, and the academic blogosphere bulged with conjecture concerning what lay behind the murders. The decline of the family, enabling campus environments, trans fats, class conflict, heteronormative culture, steroids, postmodernism, and Geraldo Rivera's moustache all found advocates. The concept of innocent until proven guilty collapsed under the tsunami of opinion making. Ambiguity, nuance, and complexity earned little favor with the pundit posse. The ideals of the classroom—critical thinking, clear-headed reflection, fair-minded inquiry—all took a backseat to flip speculation. It seemed to Ramble as if the self-appointed mavens of criminal and societal behavior would agree

wholeheartedly with pro basketball's Charles Barkley's pronouncement: "I am not a role model."

But, like Sir Charles, did they really have a choice in that regard?
Ramble wasn't so sure.

It seemed to him that much of what faculty members did day by
day unavoidably tagged them as role models. Were not professors attempting to model the educated person? The values trumpeted as outcomes of a liberal education? Approaches to knowledge and scholarship
associated with one's academic discipline? Professionalism in a career?
Being a good citizen? Ramble wondered what were the dimensions and
opportunities of being a role model for students? How did a professor
go about being a role model in the classroom and outside it? How
should a professor prepare to be an on-campus role model? What were
the traps and pitfalls of any professor's attempt at being a role model
for students? What the hell had Leo's absent-minded mouse clicking
called up on his computer screen?

"Leo, are you ready for that kind of dating?"

"Criminently, Buffalo Bob." Leo ogled photo ads of potential Har-
monic Academic Relationships. He clicked off the popup screen reluctantly and read aloud from a blog site titled Välkommen Voicings.

> Norman Cady's eventual guilt or innocence notwithstanding, he repre-
> sents a growing group of students who challenge the concept of residen-
> tial higher education and threaten the majority of Välkommen U
> students who deserve to have their choice to live on campus as full
> members of the academic community honored and safeguarded. We
> cannot stand by and watch our campus fall into the same misdirection
> as so many other liberal arts colleges, now but distant memories in
> academe.

"Isn't that Luella DeiSel's blog thing?" Ramble asked.

"Who else." Leo examined the bottom of his mouse, picking at a
significant shred of dust and sandwich crumb buildup. "You know
what I find so interesting?"

"What's so interesting?"

"How do these scribbling professors find the time for all this blogging and tweeting crap? It has to eat up one's waking hours to manage

these sites. And how do they come up with names for these blogs? Sort of reminds me of citizen band radio days."

"What was your handle again?" Ramble recalled Leo's brief phase in the early 1970s as Slapbutt Scholar Stud. It had drawn a strange reaction from many of the long-haul truckers on the highway.

"I would opt for a dual blogging," Leo said, ignoring Ramble's question. "I favor a night and day approach. Perhaps peevedprofessor and pissedprofessor would do nicely as my blog titles."

"Cocktail hour being the dividing line?"

"You know me well, Ramble."

Leo went back to working his computer mouse. "Here's a good example of an academic blog genre. Permit me to summarize from a recent post on ScienceGuy. He has several entries on a general theme: *himself*. In this particular posting, "Every Which Way I Lose," we are informed our merry blogger has just secured a tenured position at a good university. He received an offer right after grad school but couldn't accept because his wife didn't see a good fit for her interests. Since that fateful moment, he has been plunged into a deep funk about his marriage, his career, his very deepest self-identity."

"My God, Leo. Tell me more."

"Just so, my friend."

Leo squinched his eyes, battling with the small print. Ramble had attempted to explain how the zoom on Leo's browser worked but to no avail.

"Let's see," Leo said. "We get a quick but intimate summary of his childhood and teenage years, as well as traumas of early adulthood and graduate school. He informs us how conflicted he is about being a father and professor at the same time. He wonders, of course, could he possibly combine all the roles successfully, and still have time to become a gourmet cook?"

"I hope he has an online support group."

"Yes," Leo scrolled down another column of the site. "He is a member of several support groups for a variety of issues. I shall not burden you with all his links."

"We've all felt his pain at one time or another, haven't we?"

"Speak for yourself." Leo glanced over his shoulder at Ramble, adjusting his reading glasses. "The object of our interest tells us he loves his new faculty position. Everything *seems* good. He *guesses* he is fulfilled academically." Leo hunched forward, exhaling a theatrical sigh. "But life is never simple, is it? In the midst of his reach for the happy life, he lists everything that might possibly go awry. He provides us with a virtuoso display of second-guessing. I can only imagine what it would be like for him to win a Lotto jackpot."

"Be not so cynical, Leo," Ramble urged. "It's the age of public self-analysis, of self-promotion, of intimate sharing. Why expect our colleagues to be so different?" Of course Ramble wondered why anyone in an academic position would engage in such a cheesy public display. Ramble was glad he had grown up in an age when football coaches and politicians didn't cry at the drop of a hat.

Leo rummaged in a desk drawer and pulled out a bag of yogurt-flavored cranberry bits. He poured Ramble a handful. "On the upside, I have found some damn interesting casual thinking-out-loud in these blogs."

Ramble found it hard to imagine the highest echelon of literature scholars in his field spending their off hours blogging. "The top dogs in your field do this thing?"

"Not really. But it's nice to get a few less-exalted takes on new research and publications. If you can cut through all the crap and scholarly narcissism, some interesting thoughts and discussions emerge. The problem is there are so many blogs, portals, carnivals, cyber birdcalls, and whatever else, it's hard to see the forest for the trees. Democracy always has its limits."

"Neurotic academic bloggers as protected hires, Leo?" Ramble asked. To his way of thinking, Mr. ScienceGuy and his ilk wouldn't be on a final list of candidates for any academic position. Frankly, he would advise candidates about blogging and Facebook sort of things. If the information were out there, he thought, it damn well might count in hiring. Maybe it should.

Ramble closed his eyes and drew a deep breath. It felt good to be back on campus. He had appealed his banishment to the president's legal adviser and regained his full privileges. Ramble had missed his students and give-and-takes with Leo and other colleagues. What a change from his funk at the beginning of the semester. He found it hard to imagine being anything else than a professor. Why the hell was that?

"If you had to do it all over again, Leo, would you—"

"What? Be a college professor?"

"Yeah."

"It's simple. What other profession would allow us to be the clowns we really are and get paid for it?" Leo pressed his fingers together, his eyes wide. "Why, that's perfect grist for my dual blog."

The campus bell sounded 5:00 p.m. Ramble glanced at his watch. Leo shut down his computer. "Let's adjourn to a nice dining spot with appropriate cocktails. I can practice tweeting or something."

CHAPTER 18

Leo didn't care much for sushi but loved the price and heft of the cocktails at Kato's Japanese Restaurant. He also liked Kazumi-san, the attractive owner, who in turn thought Leo quite cute and amusing. For that reason alone, Leo made Kato's his home away from home. Kazumi, who most certainly had been a stunning beauty in her youth, fussed over Leo and prepared him specialty items—some of which required deep draughts of his cocktail to properly savor the cuisine and please his hostess. Fortunately, Ramble loved Japanese food, and he was willing to help his friend in those moments of acute culinary distress—much to the delight of the sushi chef, Yamata-san.

"Sometimes I feel like a dog underneath your table," Ramble informed Leo.

As Kazumi returned to the kitchen, Ramble inhaled a major portion of his friend's aji no tataki, a small, silvery Spanish mackerel, chopped up raw with a ginger garnish. Yamata giggled at the high jinks as he sliced into a chunk of deep red tuna.

"Such a comment requires no response, Fido." Leo's chopstick blocked Ramble's grab for a deep-fried aji carcass and bones. He liked those.

Angela hurried into the restaurant and stood next to Leo's chair.

"You can order this beautiful young woman some of the same," Leo instructed Ramble, accepting a hug from Angela. "Maybe she'll share it with you."

"I'm glad you could make it." Ramble poured Angela some of his hot sake into a delicate lacquered cup. "I thought you had a late meeting."

"The all-university meeting you were supposed to attend?" Angela held the sake cup to her lips, and tipped up her delicate chin to swallow. "It didn't take as long as advertised. You missed some very interesting news."

"Darn. I forgot all about it."

"Sure you did." Angela refilled her sake cup. "Along with 80% of the faculty."

"That bad, huh?" Leo inspected the serving plate Kazumi placed in front of him containing two thin slices of white fish on rice, topped with tiny bits of green onion and Japanese red pepper and grated radish. Kazumi bowed slightly to Angela and brushed her hand across Leo's shoulder.

"It's halibut, Leo-san," Kazumi informed him and waited for him to taste it.

"It looks sooo tasty, Kazumi-san." Leo managed a weak smile. "So *yoshi*."

"*Yoshi?*" Kazumi gave him a strange look and a quick bow. She returned to the kitchen, staring over her shoulder at Leo. He had taken up Japanese, using a cartoon-illustrated paperback text to learn the language. The back pages contained cutout words he could paste on objects around his apartment. The last time Ramble had visited, little yellow strips of paper littered Leo's apartment, taped to appliances, chairs, windows, and just about any other surface and object available.

"I believe the correct word is *oishi*, Leo." Angela reached across to snag the remaining piece of his sushi. She had spent a year on a faculty exchange to Japan. "It's cute, though, your learning Japanese."

Leo ordered another cocktail.

"At least you didn't tell Kazumi the halibut tasted like an airplane or something like that."

"Thanks, Ramble." Leo gave a warning look to a smirking Yamata behind the sushi counter. "You were saying, Angela?"

"Our president has informed us the merry good ship Välkommen has sailed slightly off course into dangerous waters." Angela sipped more of her sake. The gloss on her lips nearly matched the deep red enamel of the sake cup. "According to Dingkudgel, the bad publicity about the murders has slowed applications for next year to a crawl, and several parents have pulled their kids out of school. Of course, we were already lacking bodies—warm ones, that is. We were down in enrollments for this year and for next fall before all this happened. In addition to our enrollment troubles, the all-important community funding sources are disappearing."

"I assume the president is especially concerned about our dear university friend Bruce Haney." Leo glanced at the kitchen doors. Kazumi had yet to return. "I wish I knew more about that guy."

"The president painted a dire budget picture," Angela said. "He sounded a warning, that's for sure."

"Sometimes a dire budget picture escapes the descriptive talents of even the most gifted administrator." Ramble thought of his attempts to discuss budgets with the English department. Like the pot of gold at the end of the rainbow, his faculty often assumed as gospel the idea that all administrators had some stash of dollars hidden in their budgets.

"I take it dear Dingkudgel had his solutions ready." Leo plucked the cherry from his Manhattan and popped it into his mouth.

"He did indeed," Angela replied. "He mentioned his pet projects again—new graduate degrees, the distance learning thing, and big-time sports teams."

"Doesn't he know that'll just dig us in deeper?" Ramble asked. "It's not just a matter of public opinion. The startup for all these programs will be huge."

"Just think of the cost for football helmets." Leo drank the last drops left of his cocktail. "Then you have to spend a bunch recruiting enough empty heads to fill them."

Ramble raised an eyebrow in Leo's direction.

"Sorry, Ramble. I forgot you played."

"Merega Raund and Stanley Robin really went after Dingkudgel," Angela said. "They had some pretty strong things to say about his plans."

"Don't they always." Ramble said. "But all in all, I'd say more power to them."

The idea of marching side by side with that particular dissenting pair hardly filled Ramble with soaring enthusiasm. But the angles Dingkudgel had chosen to play didn't make much sense. "I expect Merega and Stanley may want to watch their step. I don't think Dingkudgel takes criticism well. Come to think of it, I've never heard him admit to the slightest mistake."

"You want to know the worst?" A slight blush edged across Angela's cheekbones, probably owing to the sake. Ramble felt a small thump in his chest watching her. "We'll be meeting next Friday afternoon and Saturday morning." Angela said. "Our president feels we need motivation."

"What?" Ramble and Leo spoke almost in unison, although the latter's enunciation suffered from the effects of a second Manhattan.

"At Haney's counsel, President Dingkudgel has secured the services of none other than Barney Buhtzkis, noted intellectual and ex-NFL noseguard."

"I believe Mr. Buhtzkis prefers 'Boomer' to Barney." Ramble said.

Leo clapped his hands together. "What an inspired choice to spark our collective spirit. Let's see. There is no 'I' in TEAM."

"No pain, no gain," Ramble rejoined.

"Keep your focus." Leo punched his fist in the air.

"It's a game of inches." Angela caught the spirit.

Leo missed a beat but recovered quickly. "Aahhh . . . It's not the size of the dog in the fight . . ."

"It's the size of the fight in the dog." Ramble spun his chair toward Angela.

Angela jumped up, letting go with a cheer. "Motivation. Inspiration. Perspiration."

"Go, Team, Go!" Ramble and Leo sang out.

Following apologies to Kazumi and the three other patrons at the sushi bar, conversation turned to other topics. As Ramble half listened, he thought about Dingkudgel and the somewhat odd turn of events. Things didn't add up.

After giving Angela some help in finishing her sake, Leo embarked on a demonstration of his newly acquired Japanese language skills. He pointed at various objects, identifying each with a Japanese word. Chairs, tables, doors, chopsticks, shoes, and whatever else in sight proved fair game for his budding vocabulary. By the time Leo progressed to arms, legs, eyes, ears, and other body parts, a small cluster of waiters and kitchen employees had gathered, whispering and gesturing to each other. Little gusts of mirth escaped Yamata's nose as he tended to a plate of sashimi. Kazumi stood a few feet away, her eyes betraying only a hint of what seemed to be pained amazement.

"O-can-jo, o-ku-de-sighed." Leo said to Yamata.

"Kumbaya, Leo-san." Yamata sliced some tuna for a roll. "You speak many languages."

"I think you meant Okanjo wo kudasai, Leo-san." Kazumi signaled the cashier.

"Of course. That's it! Check, please." Leo rose unsteadily from his seat at the sushi bar. He bowed to Kazumi, and made a great show of rubbing his stomach. He said something that sounded like, "Goatcheese-so Sammy Sosa."

Kazumi looked back and forth between Leo and Yamata. The sushi chef merely shook his head. Angela laid her head on the counter, her shoulders shaking from a fit of the giggles. "No more, Leo, please."

"Say good night, Leo." Ramble steered his friend to the door. "In English, please."

CHAPTER 19

The first hour of Ramble's class had gone nowhere. His honors students slumped in their chairs around the seminar table, silent, eyes downcast. The excitement of class meetings held before Ramble's banishment from campus had evaporated; the students' interest in creating a different path for their study of literature had vanished. Reports on projects fell on deaf ears, and the class limped through a discussion on the day's reading assignment. Even Melody, the enemy of conversational dead space, somehow showed no zest for classroom confrontation.

"Come on, people. It's like *The Night of the Living Dead* here." Ramble leaned back from the table, prepared to wait as long as it took for someone to respond. He studied his class list, checking off Marissa Vargas and Kevin Connolly as absent. After a long, uncomfortable moment of silence, Josh shifted in his chair, apparently ready to speak. He took a deep breath but said nothing. Several students studied their fingernails. Others gazed at the seminar table surface in front of them with great intensity. Some rearranged their books and notes. A few practiced thoughtful expressions and poses.

Finally, Jessica Chen, a very promising student in Ramble's opinion, placed her hands on the table surface, palms down, ready to say something. "We had two sessions while you were gone. I was really proud of how we got along without you for most of the time. But, last week's session . . ."

"Had its ups and downs." Amy Klein finished her friend's thought. Students around the table nodded in agreement.

"Did you enjoy Professor Agee's visit?" Ramble hadn't seen Sam Agee yet, much less thanked him for taking over two sessions of the honors class. Sam was too wrapped up in the fight for Nadine Watkins's appointment.

"We liked him just fine," Amy said. "But he couldn't make it to the last week's class."

"So what did you do?"

"Professor Agee had asked us if we'd read any African American mystery writers yet. We hadn't, because our list for the semester isn't complete." Amy fiddled with her earrings, undecided if she should continue. "He told us to each bring the name of one African American mystery author to the next meeting."

"Yeah, well, that was just the start of things, wasn't it? Since Professor Agee couldn't be at the class, we never made it to discussing the African American mystery writers." Jelani Saunders, the only African American student in the class, hadn't said much in discussions, but his written assignments were well reasoned, and Ramble liked the young man's writing style—straightforward, to the point, no fooling around.

"We just made a list of the writers, and then my fellow class members decided to move on." Jelani said. "So what's new?"

"Come on, Jelani, that's not fair," Amy said.

"How do you know what's fair for me?"

"Why didn't you say something?" Melody asked.

Jelani rolled his eyes.

Ramble watched as most members of the class shifted uncomfortably in their chairs, attempting to avoid engagement with Jelani.

"It's like if there's only me, you all don't have to pay any attention to what I might think," Jelani said.

"But we've asked you for your perspective lots of times," Amy persisted. "I think you're selling us short."

"Yeah. 'Let's ask the token what he thinks. He'll set us straight on what all the African Americans are thinking.' Like you really believe I belong here."

"What has got into you?" Ray Kent asked, his face reflecting surprise and concern. Ramble had seen Ray and Jelani hanging around together after class. They seemed like good friends. "I know things can't be easy around here for you," Ray continued, "but this class is different. Isn't it?"

"Whatever you say, Ray." Jelani stared down at his notebook, drawing jagged lines on the cover with his ballpoint pen. "I guess I must be imagining all the crap that goes down at this school."

"I think I can understand a little of what you're saying," Amy said.

"It's not like we skate by here," Starry added.

"My soul mates?" Jelani said. "Give me a break."

Ramble could sense things going very quickly downhill. His experiences in life, long talks with Sam Agee, all that he'd ever studied, as well as what he perceived as good intentions, didn't give him much confidence about the unfolding situation. How much did he really know about what a student like Jelani had to face at the university? Ramble recalled Jelani coming into the office to talk about a draft assignment. Ramble's attempts to offer criticism and suggestions—similar, he thought, to what any student would expect from him as the professor—seemed to upset Jelani and build a wall between them. Ramble had no idea at that time what he'd done wrong. Worse yet, he still didn't know enough about the young man as an individual or enough about the problems African American students faced to make sense of the situation and help resolve it. Good intentions didn't carry much weight and seldom bridged the gaps of understanding. Teaching strategies and techniques wouldn't automatically guarantee success.

As for the immediate situation—should he interrupt and try to steer the class toward calmer waters? Was there some sort of assignment he could give to focus a discussion on Jelani's concerns? What did the young man want to happen? Ramble needed to do something.

"If I can cut into this conversation, I'd like to make a few suggestions." Ramble waited until he received a general signal of approval from the class. Several nodded in assent.

Ramble hoped he could do the right thing.

"I don't think I'd be doing my job very well if I let us skip away from this conversation. But, if you don't mind my saying so, I don't think we're heading in a direction that befits us as honors students, as serious learners. Now, in that rarified context, let me ask you, where should we go from here, and how should we proceed?"

"Jelani?" Ramble waited for the young man to meet his gaze. "From what I've read of your assignments, and from your contributions to class discussion in regard to our readings, you are an intellectually talented young man." Ramble paused and gave the other students a wry glance. "Of course, the rest of you aren't exactly a bunch of schlunks."

Laughter and grins flickered through the seminar room.

"Uh-oh. I think our esteemed professor is about to drop the other shoe," Jelani said.

"Nothing so bad, Jelani," Ramble replied. "But I need you and each student to do something before our next meeting."

"And that is?" Jelani asked.

"First of all, I'd like you and a couple of other volunteers to come back next week with some specific examples—drawn from your reading of African American mystery writers—of what we might call subtle racial slights and actions."

"I don't get what you mean," Melody said.

"It's like when people ask me where I'm from," Jessica chimed in. "And I love it when they tell me I speak English so well."

"Well, you're on the right track there," Ramble said.

"It's like being invisible," Jelani said, his voice barely above a whisper.

Ramble let Jelani's comment linger in the room for a time before breaking the silence. "I'll arrange to have Sam Agee meet with you and your group, Jelani."

Ramble hoped to hell Sam wouldn't be too busy. He also needed to call on some of his colleagues to help him define the focus of the assignment.

"I'm on it," Jelani said.

"As for the rest," Ramble said, "I'm going to ask you each to read one of the African American mystery novelists with an eye on how they describe their interactions with Whites and how these interactions mirror what we've met up with today in class."

His students seemed to be enthusiastic about the assignment, and Ramble allowed them a few minutes to organize their research groups and breathed a sigh of relief. Maybe he'd done the right thing and taken advantage of a teaching moment. But Jessica Chen punctured his bubble.

"Professor Ramble, I don't know if we want to go here, but Elena and I have a question."

During the previous few minutes for organizing groups, Jessica and Elena Garcia had spent the time in an earnest two-way conversation. Damn it. Ramble should have known to widen the franchise and allow students to pursue the topic in regard to other ethnicities. Why wouldn't Jessica or Elena feel a similar isolation and experience the same subtle racism as Jelani?

"It seems I have neglected to extend the opportunities for students regarding this assignment, haven't I?" Ramble watched as Jessica and Elena affirmed his tardy realization by a pair of pleasant but knowing smiles.

"I guess we never stop learning, do we?" Ramble said and called for a renewed discussion of the assignment with an expanded sweep of territory.

CHAPTER 20

"Anything else we need to settle?" Ramble asked the class following a five-minute break. Things seemed to be cool now, and he hoped the honors class would be ready to tackle an assignment he'd made before his two-week forced sabbatical.

After some pleading on Ramble's part, the class had agreed to read Herman Melville's novella *Benito Cereno*. It qualified in Ramble's mind as a mystery, and to be honest, he really wanted to see how an honors class of students would handle one of the classic writers of the nation's nineteenth century. The students had teased him good-naturedly about his not "letting go," but most had already read Edgar Allan Poe, the acknowledged father of modern mystery.

He posed an opening question. "Is it fair to use *Benito Cereno* as a mystery?"

"Professor Ramble?"

"Yes, Elena?"

"We did start discussing this last time, but we didn't get very far."

"OK. Let's hear about it."

Having used the novella several times over the years, Ramble could hazard a guess why the class may not have been successful. Melville had constructed a complex story, laden with issues about race and slavery. Generations of students and literary critics had squabbled over the meaning of the novella. Also, Melville's focus on race and slavery and the literary camouflage he applied to plot and character proved difficult for students and led to some emotional reactions.

"A couple of class members really got their noses out of joint." Elena said. She pointed to where Kevin Connolly and Marissa Vargas usually sat. "It'll be a little hard to recap the events, but maybe somebody can fill in the blanks."

Jelani rubbed his fledgling goatee. "As you probably intended, *Benito Cereno* had us all uptight. Marissa got frustrated at something, so she left the class."

"You were sort of picking on her, Jelani," Amy Klein said.

Jelani waved his paperback copy of *Benito Cereno*. "First thing she said was how Melville was always trashing her people. The story wasn't really about that. I don't think she'd read it carefully, and I tried to tell her so. Maybe I didn't do a very good job, but next thing I know, she's running out of the room crying and yelling at us."

"I don't disagree with what you were saying to Marissa, but it came out the wrong way." Ray Kent said.

"I'll wrong-way you tonight playing hoops, Ray."

A grin spread across Jelani's face as he looked across the table at his friend. The two young men hung around together on campus, so Ramble knew it wasn't any sort of a confrontation. Marissa, a first-generation college student whose parents had come to the United States from Colombia, didn't seem a likely candidate for the sort of behavior Jelani described. Like Melville's story, Ramble knew the answers to what had happened in the class had to lie deeper. Once again, he probably knew less about his students than he should.

"I think it's more like she's caught in the middle," Jessica Chen said.

Elena gave her friend a strange look. "Caught in the middle of what?"

"Well, before Marissa comes here to class, she has to deal with all the anti-immigrant talk."

"*She* has to deal with all that anti-immigrant talk?" Elena affected an expression of wonderment. "Marissa can trace her ancestry all the way back to Spanish nobility. I think she's got other reasons for why she read the story the way she did. I sure didn't identify with the Spanish captain."

Jessica seemed confused, as did the rest of the class. Elena was one of a small number of student advisees assigned to Ramble in his role as department chair. He knew her background. Her Mexican-born parents, from the state of Morelos, and now citizens of the United States, lived and worked in a growing community of Mexican Americans along Lake Street in Minneapolis. Elena's father, the successful owner of a small restaurant and a video store, had often taken a leadership role in defending the civil rights of his community members. It made sense to Ramble that Elena might untangle the motives behind Marissa Vargas's behavior as she did. But things seemed to be going in a harmful direction, and Ramble thought it important to call a halt. Jelani beat him to it.

"I don't think we should be talking about Marissa and what she might have thought when she's not here," Jelani said, and other members of the class seemed to agree.

"Fair enough. But let me make a point." Elena put both hands flat on the table surface and straightened her arms. "The point is that sometimes all the bad things people say and the way they act aren't the only things that can get someone—like myself—all stressed out and feeling like an outsider."

"I'm sorry, Elena, but what are you saying?" Jessica asked her friend. "What am I missing?"

"I'm saying it gets you down. It hurts to be on the spot all the time."

"You mean like me being the only Black student in my social inequalities class?" Jelani punched one fist into the other. "Or how about when we discuss slavery in my history class? Sometimes I feel like a penguin at the zoo."

"That's it," Elena said. "Or how about being the one a teacher asks, 'What do you think about that, Elena?' I know it's good to have all these classes that deal with race, gender, diversity, and all that. But give me a break. And I mean *me*."

"So how do we avoid hurting people and still have good classes and good discussions?" Starry asked. "It's not like we can avoid it all."

The class broke into conversations and spent the next 15 minutes trying to answer Starry's question. As he listened, Ramble wondered how he would have handled the troubling, delicate situation the class had experienced without him. Should he have anticipated new danger spots with the assignment—different from what he had previously learned about through experience teaching *Benito Cereno*? Maybe so. What could he and the students do now to fix things? How could they all learn something of substance from the incident? Were things always so damn complicated? Of course they were.

Something else bugged Ramble. He should have put himself through some sort of pre-fall semester training. Even at this late stage in his career, he had an obligation to work on the fundamentals of classroom teaching and to ask some hard questions about the quality and substance of his course objectives and assignments. Just like the professional baseball teams that went through the early weeks of spring training each year—working on the basics like run downs, base running, sacrifice bunts—Ramble needed to get back to the basics and fine-tune his teaching. Things changed in the classroom, he knew, and sometimes much quicker than anyone expected.

After the discussion had begun to run its course, Ramble asked, "So, did I miss any other excitement?" He smiled at the class, trying to loosen them up. They didn't budge, except for Melody.

"Professor Ramble, I hate to bring this up, but as we all have noticed by the lack of commentary from that direction," Melody pointed to an empty chair on the other side of the table, "Kevin Connelly isn't here in class today."

Melody had that impish look on her face. Ramble imagined her playing the role of one of Shakespeare's forest sprites without blinking an eye. Why hadn't Kevin Connelly shown up for class today? He'd seen Kevin walking to the student union earlier.

"Is there anything I should know?" Ramble looked at Melody for an answer.

"I should probably tell you about it." Ray interrupted. "Kevin and I had a little disagreement."

"A little disagreement?" Melody rolled her eyes. "More like a mega spat."

Ray ignored Melody. "I like Kevin, but we don't agree on much."

Ramble liked Kevin as well. He had a sharp, discerning mind, and he argued his positions with the same skills he used to good effect as captain of the university's debate team. He intimidated some students in the honors class with his debater's mien and an acid wit, but the young man added an important voice to class discussions.

"After the blowup with Marissa, Kevin told us he expected she'd throw a hissy fit," Melody said.

Ray gestured toward Starry. "She called him on his use of terminology. Kevin blew her off and jumped into his wannabe teacher thing."

"He didn't have to be like that," Starry shifted uncomfortably in her chair. "He said all of us are paying the price for what he imagines about political correctness and multicultural classroom stuff."

Ramble had his own doubts about a few aspects of multiculturalism. It seemed like some of his colleagues had gone too far with their enthusiasm for the multicultural curriculum. He didn't think most Välkommen U students entered the college classroom with a great fund of academic experience and background understanding so they could easily participate in the academics' give-and-take on multiculturalism. It also meant that faculty, often isolated from one another by disciplinary boundaries and closeted in their individual classrooms, might create an environment filled with a welter of multicultural approaches and theories that would make students uncomfortable and confused. Would students feel pressured? Elena and Jelani apparently felt that way. Why not the other students? Would they retreat from discussions? Would they resent the whole enterprise? Many probably would. Worse yet, most undergraduates, intent on making a good grade, would walk a well-worn pragmatic path: "Don't think about it, just let the professors hear what they want to hear." As Ramble moved to stand at a row of windows facing the quad, he didn't feel ready to offer a wise, comforting summary to his students. He needed more information.

"How did you respond to Kevin?" Ramble asked.

"It wasn't easy," Ray said. The other students nodded and smiled. "Kevin wanted to debate, of course."

"But what was his point?" Ramble didn't think Kevin meant any harm. He simply didn't see himself as others in the class did.

"I don't like the way he goes about things, but Kevin did make me think." Amy doodled on her notebook for a moment.

"He said it's ridiculous to erase the classics of Western civilization from our reading and study in literature. He said most college students don't have any experience reading those books and stuff, so why does it make sense to substitute things that are only a small part of our overall history and culture? Most of us in this class have read some of those classics in Western literature by now, but do the majority of high school and college students have the same opportunity? Kevin says no. Does it make sense to leave out Shakespeare, Jane Austin, or Tolstoy and substitute something else just because it's supposed to be multicultural? I don't know. Maybe what I'm thinking is that all these writers deal with some pretty big themes. Why shouldn't we read the best?" Amy put up a hand to cover her mouth. "Sorry. I didn't mean to go on like that."

"So you're saying I should pack up my Richard Wright, Ralph Ellison, and Alice Walker? When do you learn about my tradition?" Jelani made sharp lines across his notebook with his pen. "When do you learn about the rest of us here in America?"

"I understand what you're saying, Jelani, but Kevin seemed to think that the classics should be a perfect take-off point for any student." Josh came aboard the discussion looking anxious, but apparently excited about what he had to say. "Remember, Kevin was arguing that the things the classics deal with are universal—you know—war, death, justice, and things like that."

"Those aren't always my universals," Jessica cut in.

"What's that supposed to mean?" Ray Kent frowned at his classmate.

"It sounds like Kevin identified a serious issue." Ramble returned to sit at the seminar table.

"I don't know," Melody said. "I go from class to class, and I can't seem to put everything I hear into something that makes sense for me."

A number of the students agreed with a suddenly thoughtful Melody. Ramble urged her to spell out her misgivings.

"Sometimes I feel like I'm being forced to accept some recipe. It doesn't seem much different from memorizing periodic elements in chemistry. And you know what?" Melody leveled an accusing gaze at Ramble.

"What?"

"I think you faculty need to talk things out and come up with a better plan."

Ramble allowed that Melody had a point. Of course she had never sat through a faculty meeting on a topic like multiculturalism. Reluctantly, Ramble checked the clock on the opposite wall. He had a late-afternoon department meeting scheduled but knew the subject at hand required more discussion. "So why isn't Kevin here today?"

"Things got a bit out of hand when Kevin tried to divide us up into debate teams." Josh looked for confirmation from his fellow students.

"I can imagine," Ramble said. "So what happened?"

"Kevin got in touch with his version of the feminine side," Melody purred, drawing smiles from the other students. "Poor baby had a hissy fit."

CHAPTER 21

Saturday Morning

Ramble watched Barney "Boomer" Buhtzkis exit the podium in a huff and labor to cross the stage, massive shoulders hunched, beach ball abdomen hanging forlornly over his belt, skinny knock-kneed legs spavined by too many operations. No roars from the crowd, no orchestrated cheers of "Boomer, Boomer" as in the days of his gridiron glory—nothing but a scattering of sympathetic hand claps from faculty members seated in the Välkommen U conference center. Only when President Dingkudgel, standing in the wings, attempted to offer a congratulatory handshake to the pro football linebacker legend did the man destined for the pigskin Hall of Fame regain some semblance of his former self.

Buhtzkis shouldered aside President Dingkudgel like a pesky undersized wide receiver and dealt a thunderous forearm shiver to the auditorium wall, leaving a gaping hole clear through the plaster surface to the studs. The crushing, helmet-rattling maneuver drew gasps of amazement from faculty members seated in the front rows. Ramble couldn't help but be impressed. After extricating his elbow and most of his arm from the cavity he'd made in the wall, the man who had averaged four sacks per game in his final season for the Minnesota Vikings emitted one of his famous on-field bellows, followed by his specially choreographed, celebratory dance—the Boomer Boogie. Ramble wondered how any true Viking fan could forget old number 56? The elemental Boomer Buhtzkis had returned full force.

"You psycho book huggers! You chalkdust zombies!" Buhtzkis screamed at the professors. "You twittering tweedy tweets."

An enraged Buhtzkis ran to center stage again, windmilling his brawny arms, roaring, grunting, hurling what the learned audience of academics (with a nod to the footballer's alliterative attack) later could only explain as painful philippic and scathing scurrility.

Ramble listened attentively as Buhtzkis snarled at the audience, "You nerd wimps don't need my motivation coaching. You need a swift kick in your academic asses. I'll never send one of my kids here."

With that threat, Buhtzkis, footballer-cum-motivator-team builder-inspirational speaker hobbled off the stage to a hastily organized cocksure chorus of "Bye Bye Boomer" led by Merega Raund and Stanley Robin. The majority of faculty, unmoved and insulted by Buhtzkis's attempts to raise their collective spirits, roundly applauded the singers (once assured the ferocious linebacker had slammed out of the building).

Having learned of Dingkudgel's plans for a three-part all-day faculty service assembly, Ramble had arrived a tad late, missing the preludes to Boomer's tumultuous leave taking. He spied Leo in one of the back rows, wrapped in a dark trench coat, wearing sunglasses, a checked wool Trilby hat, and sporting a false mustache. Ramble walked up the stairs and squeezed into a seat next to his friend.

"Phone call for Inspector Clouseau." Ramble held out his cell phone as a joke.

Leo put a finger to his lips. "Ah yes. That would be me." He worked at tapping down the false mustache where it had begun to peel back.

Some of the faculty would not have welcomed Leo's presence at the meeting, thus his attempt at subterfuge. He had no right to attend meetings as a retiree. Besides, he'd always caused a ruckus in years gone by if Ramble's memory served him right. Why Leo wanted to attend a university meeting in the first place would make for a whole other subject.

The auditorium still resounded with taunts and invective. Rarely had Ramble witnessed such bad blood and rebelliousness among his fellow professors. The bad publicity and scandal generated by the campus murders had the academics off balance, agitated, and at that moment, looking for trouble. The president's Management by Vision crusade had minimal support. Faculty preferred to keep their small university intact, without significant changes. Ramble pretty much agreed and joined the others in seeing the president's motivation session for what it was—a jump-off point toward an unfamiliar, unwanted future for Välkommen U.

"It all started when Boomer racked up the first PowerPoint slide," Leo said. "It had those inspirational quotes from Hugh Hefner, Ivana Trump, Vince Lombardi, Dr. Phil, and Zig Ziglar. You know—the usual suspects. But the best one was from the *One Minute Manager* guy, Ken Blanchard."

"What was it?"

"Don't quack like a duck; soar like an eagle."

"What?"

"Exactly." Leo took off his sunglasses and blinked his eyes. "Boomer puts up all these dopey quotes on the screen, and then he wants everyone to get in huddles and discuss this lame-brained Mickey Mouse motivation crap. Can you imagine asking faculty, no less a bunch of humanities professors, to *huddle?*"

"It's asking for trouble, I admit." Ramble saw Angela a couple of rows down, smiling in his direction. He waved for her to join him.

"The philosophers and the literature folks had a ball with the 'quack like a duck' thing," Leo said. "Those crazies in the theater department started flapping and soaring around. Then everybody started quacking. Poor Boomer didn't have a clue."

Angela worked her way down the row of auditorium seats toward Ramble and Leo. She leaned behind Ramble and touched Leo's arm. "I like your disguise, Inspector."

Leo sighed. "Angela, tell Ramble what Boomer did after the flight of the ducks."

Angela's eyes filled with excitement. "Boomer yelled out a bunch of numbers and colors. I think it must have been some sort of linebacker's flashback. Then he charged after that mime guy in the theater department.

"Russell Sprute?"

"Yes. He was having a great old time doing some sort of duck thing, and Boomer damn near caught him with a flying tackle right in the middle of the theater department discussion group."

"You mean *huddle*, don't you?" Leo said.

Ramble watched President Dingkudgel step to the microphone. He looked calm. A man in charge. Undeterred, despite the ongoing hoopla over Boomer Buhtzkis's failed motivational mission to academe.

"May I please have your attention?" With a pleasant smile on his face, Dingkudgel waited for the faculty to hush and listen, appropriating several seconds to make eye contact with individuals in the audience.

The meeting had been billed as one for which business-casual dress would be appropriate—a borrowing from the corporate world that had absolutely no meaning for college faculty. Ramble could attest from his own view of professorial fashion that 99% of academics considered every day to be casual day. Even those from the several branches of business administration mostly ignored standards set by the corporate professionals who would someday hire Välkommen U students. Dingkudgel's idea of casual set him distinctly apart. His outfit would have been perfect for the corporate office or an executive breakfast meeting on a Friday morning. His starched blue shirt, with tab collar, worn open at the neck, accompanied by a cashmere sweater of a pinkish hue positively whispered "natural leadership." His neatly pressed, gray wool slacks fell gracefully to a luminous pair of wing-tip cordovan shoes. Dingkudgel again called for the faculty to be quiet and return to their seats, all the while maintaining a laid-back demeanor to match the intent of his outfit. He watched several professors walk in front of the stage, laughing and pointing at friends seated in the front rows.

"Please, my friends. We have other important business to deal with today." The president stepped back from the podium, waiting for gallivanting faculty members to find seats and calm down.

"Despite Mr. Buhtzkis's cutting short his presentation, let's make a positive out of a negative. In effect, we now have more time for part two of today's agenda." Ignoring the groans from many faculty members, Dingkudgel forged ahead. "We have a wonderful lunch awaiting you in rooms next door in the conference center. Remember to please take one of the envelopes my staff has ready for you at the exits. These envelopes contain your food coupons and a list of the conference rooms where you'll be assembling with department colleagues to watch our presentation on the topic 'Cyber Faculty and the Future of the University.' I'll see you back here at two o'clock for our exciting closing session. You won't want to miss that."

Ramble watched the reaction from the faculty audience. Once again they seemed unhinged, at a loss for words. Before any of the usually outspoken academics could muster some sort of reaction—even a modest protest—administrative staff swept wide open the auditorium exits, and the loudspeaker system played a peppy medley of college fight songs. Even the most resistant among the faculty arose and trudged out the open doors in the company of their peers—the promise of a free box lunch a siren call to the professors.

As the faculty cleared the auditorium, Ramble kept track of the two men remaining on the stage. Haney had a hand on the president's shoulder, drawing him close, whispering in his ear. A huge grin blossomed on Dingkudgel's face.

The English department faculty gathered in their assigned conference room. The professors munched on sandwiches, chips, pickles, and oatmeal *raison* cookies, speculating between mouthfuls about what the next hour's agenda held for them. As department chair, Ramble took it upon himself to fiddle with the TV monitor, attempting to adjust the volume for Haney's presentation. Haney's address would be telecast live to all the conference rooms, which featured huge, newly installed, wall-mounted projection screens and all the technological doodads necessary for interaction between speaker and audience. A five times larger than life image of Haney seated in the president's office before a set of expensive looking floor-to-ceiling drapes filled the screen.

"Orwell comes to campus," mused one professor.

Ramble joked with department members as he turned up the volume at the control panel. He supposed a clause in the Management by Vision plan included the broadcast of classes to off-campus sites and to multiple on-campus viewing areas. Did this mean students might not ever have to leave their dorm rooms? He didn't have proof, but thought students on the receiving end of such electronic teaching wouldn't much like it. At least he hoped so. The grainy, distorted image of the large projection screen; the echoing of voices; the technological constraints on real conversation between students and between students and teachers; the artificial, staged conditions in which any active learning would struggle to take place; and rudimentary camera work made the whole enterprise suspect in Ramble's opinion. He wondered how long it took for a professor to figure out exactly on which side the students sat in the distance learning classroom sites. Which *left* of the classroom was that again?

"Given the future direction charted for this university, which includes the creation of top-notch distance learning programs, it would be foolish to ignore the need for an enhanced and expanded teaching workforce for Välkommen University." Bruce Haney smiled into the camera, welcoming viewers to an intimate, big league conversation.

"Virtual adjuncts . . . cyber faculty . . . whatever terminology you would like to apply, are indispensable in this new world of online course work and to the degree programs now spreading throughout this nation and around the globe. We will need to recruit, train, and manage a considerable number of these virtual adjuncts in order to compete and grow in a dynamic market. We need a large aggregate of first-rate, motivated, well-trained virtual adjuncts—especially if our university is to move into highly profitable programs in which working adults can gain certification and advanced degrees." Haney allowed his audience a wry, telegenic smile. "Of course, what constitutes a high demand field for certificate awards and MA degrees is hardly static. We need to be agile, ready to replant in changing environments. Such readiness and agility require us to see adjuncts as a constantly changing resource."

"Selling coffee to the millions," came a comment from the back of the room.

"Why can't we just be one of the few, undefiled small liberal arts colleges left?" Devon McKinney, professor of British literature, buried his head in his hands. "Does every school have to be in this nasty business?"

"Online programs are well past the takeoff stage. We need to warm up our engines and be on board before it is too late," Haney continued his pitch.

Ramble and the others in the conference room groaned. Haney seemed not to cringe at the banality of his lines. "Estimates are that at least one in ten students will be taking an online course in the next year. Don't you want our students taking courses developed here and offered in our regular curriculum? In addition, why wouldn't other students in our region want to sign up for online credit-bearing courses with our respected brand name instead of some fly-by-night institution?"

"Sounds like a good way to lose faculty control of the curriculum," McKinney growled. Department members sitting near him nodded in agreement. "In my humble opinion," McKinney rattled on to his nearest colleagues, "most traditional-aged students don't have the experience or the discipline to handle any type of independent study. First-year students most certainly don't."

Haney must have anticipated the naysayers like McKinney. "I know there are those who argue younger students are not prepared for distance learning. Others will maintain that only the classroom experience provides deep learning and an enriching intellectual community. I say we cannot afford to be so pristine." Haney pointed a finger at his TV audience. "How so? you may ask."

"How so?" The faculty voices in Ramble's conference room joined in chorus.

Ramble could predict his department members' soon coming to a realization that Haney and Dingkudgel weren't blowing smoke about the new distance learning initiative or new graduate programs or, for that matter, big-time sports. Management by Vision would arrive soon with a resounding thud in the consciousness of the English department faculty.

"How so?" Haney repeated his question with a thoughtful, reflective tone and visage. "I say that Välkommen U students—if they are to be successful in the world of work and in twenty-first-century society— must have solid experience as independent learners. They must conduct independent research. They must master the intricacies of a booming Internet marketplace of knowledge, ideas, and communication. Online study is the answer."

Haney leaned forward toward the camera, drawing his unseen audience into a more intimate, if unwanted, connection. "We make a great noise in our promises of liberal education concerning the ideal of lifelong learning. I ask you, is not lifelong learning intimately connected with online learning? I think so. On all counts, we need a significant expansion in our ability to deliver the unique learning experiences and educational directions for which Välkommen U is renowned."

"A bit overstated, is that not?" Devon McKinney again resisted Haney's rhetoric. Others in the conference room mumbled their agreement. They were—after all—the English department.

Ramble feigned switching channels with the remote. "Should we see if the Twins are playing?"

Over Ramble's shoulder, Haney's bulging video image loomed in a tight camera closeup. "Our expanded adjunct professor corps will be a model of such employment in contemporary higher education. Adjuncts will be paid at a special rate per course that is 20% above that now offered. Discount group medical coverage is a possibility. Grant funding is in the works to support adjuncts' developing new courses, new materials, applied research, and travel to conferences. Finally, the university will construct the Inga Gadda Distance Learning Center. The center will be a state-of-the-art central broadcasting and computer center for our distance learning programs. In addition, the building will have an adjunct professors' office complex to provide individual spaces for each individual employed."

"I can't even fit into *my* office space," complained McKinney.

"I've been sharing the same dang office for 10 years."

"Can I be an adjunct?"

And so went reactions to the proposed adjunct cyber faculty among the members of the English department. Ramble smelled a rat. *How the hell are we going to pay for all this?* He could envision money being siphoned off from new faculty positions and no bucks for replacing retiring professors.

"A couple of proverbs may be applicable here." Printing flashed across the screen in Old English letters as Haney spoke. He read the one-liners, adding his interpretation with each.

"A candle loses nothing by lighting another candle. Välkommen University will be the same great institution, but shining in a greater, different light."

"The early bird catches the worm. We are situated in the greater Twin Cities metropolitan region—a treasure trove of well-educated, learned citizens for our virtual adjunct division of professors. We had better secure their services before others do so."

"Gosh. We wouldn't want to be a few fries short of a Happy Meal." Leo had slipped into a vacant chair near the door.

Several members of the English department gave the retired historian dirty looks.

"I'm just here for a few seconds to catch my breath, friends," Leo smiled at the professors seated near him. He massaged his chest. "My heart needs a bit of a rest before climbing all those stairs up to my broom closet."

On the TV screen, Haney rose from his chair and stood by a huge window overlooking the campus. With a dramatic sweep of his hand, he directed the viewers' attention to the quadrangle. The screen dissolved to a head shot of President Dingkudgel. He thanked Haney for his "enlightened, absolutely thrilling remarks about the university's new distance learning frontier." Then, with the school rouser sounding in the background, Dingkudgel apologized that no time remained for discussion of Haney's presentation. Without skipping a beat, the university's president called for the faculty to reassemble in the auditorium for a surprise announcement.

CHAPTER 22

"At the end of this wonderful day," President Dingkudgel announced, "it's my distinct pleasure to introduce a man of greatness, a new, key player in the Management by Vision initiative. As you know, we wish to become a major force in NCAA athletics."

A majority of the professors in the room grumbled and fidgeted in response to Dingkudgel's words. Obstinacy still prickled following Haney's explanation of the cyber faculty concept. Ramble recognized that the faculty had not lost their edge, but the president ignored the warning signs. Dingkudgel smiled broadly and placed a hand on the thick shoulder of a formidable-looking man who had marched on stage like he owned it.

"To lead us on our athletic quest, let me announce the hiring of Bobby Roy Huggy, named this morning as the first head coach of our Välkommen University Fightin' Tyrs." As Dingkudgel clapped the new football coach on the shoulder and stepped back to allow Bobby Roy access to the podium, the faculty buzzed in agitated confusion.

"Fightin' Tyrs?" Leo seemed dumbfounded. "Are we going to have a football team or a bunch of cry-baby soap opera addicts in jerseys and tight pants?"

Whatever might be the signification of the Fightin' Tyrs, the fact the university now had a football coach occupied the thoughts of most in the audience. They stared blankly ahead, assured that the president's goals for his Management by Vision initiative were, indeed, more than simply pie-in-the-sky rhetoric.

"Well, Dingkudgel and Haney didn't exactly try to slip this past us," Ramble said, watching as Haney handed Coach Huggy a spanking new white and purple football jersey, the left sleeve emblazoned with a somewhat timid-looking Norse warrior missing one hand. Word quickly circulated throughout the auditorium, thanks to the director of the School for Nordic Studies, that the wee warrior was Tyr, a one-handed Norse god, and perhaps the son of Odin, although this scholarly interpretation was the subject of much debate.

"What the hell kind of deal is this?" Leo threw his hands up in the air. "We'll have to chop some poor undergraduate's hand off to have a team mascot."

"It might save money on costuming," Ramble offered.

"But we'll only be able to sell *one* of those big rubber hands all the other teams have for their fans," Leo said. "It'll really cut down on revenues."

"I can't believe we are headed down this road of no return," Angela said. "Football, online courses, and a bunch of phony graduate programs."

Ramble watched as the press and the electronic media folks whispered into their cell phones and headsets. Given the presence of so much media firepower, the faculty should have expected something big from Dingkudgel and Haney.

"Were we in such bad shape at the start of the year?" Angela shook her head slowly. "These all seem like drastic measures for a small crisis in enrollment."

"We might lose more students than we gain if you ask me." Leo glared at the spectacle unfolding on the stage.

Reporters peppered the new football coach with questions. As Coach Huggy, Dingkudgel, and Haney spouted sports mumbo jumbo, the faculty learned that the new football coach would make more money in salary than professors in the biology, chemistry, physics, and mathematics departments put together. Ramble figured Coach Huggy's endorsements would more than dwarf the library budget, and his leased vehicles would cover most salaries in the humanities. The football guru would also receive a "loyalty bonus" of $500,000 if he stayed as head coach for two years.

By the end of the question-and-answer period, indignant faculty members were shouting questions at the men on the stage. The faculty senate president screamed for the organization's sergeant at arms to remove the media. Unfortunately, Dr. Fabio Torno, sergeant at arms and professor of romance languages and quite a gentle soul, remained glued to his chair, trembling, wide-eyed, impervious to the fervid calls for him to do something. President Dingkudgel, apparently sensing that the situation might race out of control, hustled the new football wizard out the back entrance. The media, on the lookout for something juicy, raced to catch up. In rising crescendo, faculty cries of outrage rang throughout every corner of the auditorium.

Ramble recalled what he knew of Bobby Roy Huggy's career in the world of big-time college football. Mildly successful at a number of Division 1A schools, Välkommen's new football coach rarely settled in one place for more than a couple of years. He was one of a growing breed of coaches in most major sports taking advantage of the merry-go-round of job offers from universities that for one reason or another coveted winning teams and national recognition. Bobby Roy had a pipeline into big-city high school football talent and nabbed recruits with the best of his peers. He could wrap college presidents, boosters, parents, and students around his finger. His checkered past of violations, shady deal making, and constant emigration to greener pastures didn't seem to pull him down behind the line of scrimmage when it came to career advancement. In short, to Ramble's way of thinking, Bobby Roy Huggy represented the norm of big-time college athletics.

On an educational and ethical level, Ramble wondered, why would any institution of higher education want anything to do with a high-powered athletic program, especially in football? Such programs did not pay for themselves, invited corruption, and rarely offered lasting advantages for the student-athlete participants academically, financially, or developmentally. Sports as an educational and character-building endeavor was so much crap in Ramble's book. As a football player in his college days, Ramble had seen it all. He knew firsthand what athletes in a prominent athletic program experienced. In the twenty-first-century world, what possible benefits of big-time college athletics topped the negatives? Did these modern sports programs for men and women have any justified connection with the educational missions of colleges and universities? Of course, like most Americans, those running higher education rarely judged what happened in big-time athletics on reasoned educational and ethical standards. The shocking economics of jock enterprises on 90% of college campuses appeared to have little relevance for presidents and alumni. Ramble couldn't quite put his finger on it but sensed that Välkommen U's leap into the void had a darker side.

For five more minutes, questions and acrimony about the new football team rattled off the walls. Unfortunately, not all the members of the local media had rushed off to interview the new football coach. A precious few stayed put, fascinated by the faculty members and their fury. Ramble feared the news reports and editorials about the day would escalate the damage to Välkommen U's image in the community and with students, past, present, and future. He didn't see Välkommen U students and alumni as big-time sports enthusiasts. Ramble predicted donations to the university and its programs would take a hit. So would enrollment.

Luella DeiSel seized a wireless microphone from a tangle of equipment near the podium and delivered a nonstop oration on the evils of big-time athletics to the faculty. She covered all the bases, pressed full court, and played sideline to sideline in her condemnation. At the end of her impromptu oration, an emotionally drained Luella collapsed in a nearby seat to thunderous applause from the audience. Ramble couldn't help but admire her gumption, but she could scarcely rouse herself to full vigilance as President Dingkudgel and Haney stepped back into the auditorium.

Dingkudgel looked a tad frazzled as he conferred at close quarters with his mentor at the edge of the stage. Dingkudgel cast the occasional nervous glance at the audience as Haney whispered in his ear. After a minute, Dingkudgel smiled, nodded his head, and eyed the podium microphone. Haney offered the president a hearty pat on the back and retreated backstage.

"Let me trouble you once again for your attention." Dingkudgel gulped a deep, apparently anguished breath, his eyelids fluttering with the effort. "My friends, despite all the progress we have made today in the building of a new university, I must announce a setback—momentary I assure you—but a setback nevertheless." Once again the president paused, well-manicured fingertips drumming his brow, a troubled soul searching for solace in the midst of tragedy. Ramble and the faculty leaned forward to catch the president's next words. The media stirred and shifted, excited by the prospect of something really juicy.

"Coach Huggy has made a decision to exercise an escape clause in his new contract. We are bound to honor the contract."

"What? We aren't paying him enough?" Leo looked baffled. "What the hell. Bribe him. Let poor Bobby Roy wear a Home Depot logo or a Pizza Hut sweater patch. If we're going into the big time, let's do it right."

Dingkudgel placed both hands on the podium, striking a pose drawn once again from his earlier days at the pulpit. "Our coach is our coach no longer. His alma mater has called him home to direct their football fortunes. With great regret, Coach Huggy has accepted that call to service in his home state. Despite our profound disappointment, we wish him well. Bobby Roy Huggy will always be my guy."

The media rushed at the president shouting questions, their cell phones unsheathed and crackling. The faculty sat dumbstruck, raw emotions overpowering their commitment to rational dialogue and detached analysis, their gut feelings prompting looks of defeat and utter despair at the unexpected, alarming consequences of the Management by Vision initiative.

Leo whispered to Ramble, "Our colleagues are most distraught. Some are literally *fighting Tyrs.*"

"You know what?" Angela stood with hands on hips, slowly shaking her head, her gaze on the media crowding around Dingkudgel. "All we need is another murder. That'll finish us for good."

CHAPTER 23

He worked his way up the wooden stairs to his efficiency apartment, pain shooting through his knees with every step. Dog tired. He'd finished teaching a three-hour night class, and then spent most of another hour working problems with two eager but confused students. Tomorrow he had to rise early to work as a temporary stocker at the Walmart store in Bloomington. The forty-minute commute by bus meant setting the alarm for five in the morning. His temping jobs, adjunct teaching, and part-time janitorial work for the apartment building barely covered bills and living expenses. His ex-wife still grabbed hundreds of dollars each month as part of their divorce settlement some years before. Nobody should have to live like this, he thought. But he managed a smile. Things were going to be a hell of a lot different now.

At the landing he paused for a moment and leaned his bulk against the wall. He contemplated the three remaining steps to his apartment. Placing his foot on the first step, he thought about murder victim number one: Roland Norris. If anyone ever deserved to die, that blowhard did. Burying the rock in Norris's skull had felt so good. He imagined people would have bought tickets for a chance to do the same thing.

The second step groaned under his weight. Briney Sweatman. Cut from the same rotten cloth as Norris. The dissection was a nice touch, he thought. Sweatman should have had his tongue jerked out years ago.

Music and sounds from the bar downstairs pulsated up to where he stood. So noisy was it most nights, he had to jam wads of Kleenex in his ears to get a good sleep. He'd given up trying to watch television or listen to the radio. The college kids filled the bar every day from late afternoon until closing, their shouts and laughter mixing with ear-splitting guitar riffs and all the crazy sounds of hip-hop and techno music. He ground the sole of his shoe into the scarred surface of the last stair. Abel Billings. He knew the world was a better place without that pompous idiot. The assistant dean had made his life a shambles, taken his last shred of dignity. He remembered begging for a lousy section to teach for less than $2,000 a semester while Billings smirked and made him grovel. No more of that now.

The payoff for all of it would be well earned, he thought, and the prize far outweighed any fears of being caught. He was way past any feelings of guilt. His life sucked big time. What could be worse?

Ivars Iverson remembered when Mr. Big Deal came around and made the offer. A slam dunk, he said. Ivars figured guys like that knew how to work the odds and stay out of trouble. The only loose end waited inside the apartment. Ivars had no doubt that sociopathic violence freak should be in the can. Why did Mr. Big Deal want to bring in that goofball as a partner anyway? The crazy kid beat the rap for Abel Billings. Not enough evidence, the police said. At least Norman Cady didn't squeal. Ivars wondered why not. But Cady sure as hell wouldn't get anymore chances. Ivars smiled at what he was about to do. Taking care of rubbish like Cady would be a public service, and Ivars looked forward to performing that mission. A nutcase like that could cause a load of trouble for everyone.

As he stepped inside his apartment, it didn't surprise Ivars to see Cady rummaging around inside the refrigerator for a beer. The kid had no sense of right or wrong. "Making yourself at home as usual?" Ivars asked.

"Hey . . . the poor working man returns to his hovel." Cady popped open a can of local brew and downed half of it. "Too bad you've never learned to appreciate a better beer. This stuff tastes way bad."

"Nobody asked your opinion, Cady."

Ivars tossed his book bag on the sofa. He had the throw-away handgun stowed behind one of the cushions, ready for business. Cady had his back turned as he rustled through a kitchen cabinet. Ivars seized the opportunity to reach down for his weapon. Might as well get down to it. With all the racket from the beer joint downstairs, nobody would hear a shot.

"Looking for this, Ivars?"

Ivars spun around to find Cady holding his pistol.

The bullet slicing into Ivars's chest sent him toppling backward into the tattered sofa. Slumped against the cushions, legs splayed, arms hanging limp, looking like someone settling in for a spot of late-night TV, Ivars thought about the class he'd taught that night. A session on mathematical probability no less. What were the odds of him being shot to death with his own gun? The blood spilling from a chest wound and pooling in his lap gave him an answer. *Probably pretty damn good.*

Cady used a dishrag from the sink to wipe his fingerprints off the few surfaces he'd touched. "Don't leave a single smudge behind," the man had said. Cady looked down at Ivars. *What a loser.* But nobody ever said these smart guys had any brains outside the classroom.

A floorboard creaked behind Cady.

"Put the gun down, Norman." The man stood in front of Ivars's dead body sprawled on the sofa a few feet from where Cady stood. "Don't be foolish. That's a good lad."

"Is this some kind of joke?" The man had a mean-looking gun pointed at Cady's chest.

"No joke, Norman."

The man had that hard look on his face Cady recognized so well. Five years spent in Stillwater Prison for armed assault had taught Cady a lot about that look. This guy meant business—the worst kind.

"Come on, dude." Cady hated to hear himself whine. He sounded like the chicken losers he'd bullied all his life. "I did everything you wanted. I told you I wouldn't say nothing. Dude, you don't want to do this."

"Night, night, Norman."

Cady didn't have time to remember anything, good or bad, about his twenty-seven years on earth before the silenced pistol spit a fatal ending.

The man backed over to Ivars's crumpled body. He placed the weapon in Ivars's right hand and wrapped the dead man's fingers around the stock. "Game. Set. Match," the man whispered, slowly working off the plastic glove he'd worn and observing the carnage. "Oh, my. A fatal double shooting. A fallout between coconspirators. Goodness. Gosh-o-golly. More bad publicity for Välkommen U."

"It's a twofer." Phan stood over the slack, blood-soaked bodies.

"Yep. One for you and one for me." Jarvis kneeled next to Ivars's corpse. It looked like the bodies had been around for at least a couple of days. The bar manager had come to collect the rent, and the rank odor in the apartment prompted him to use his pass key for a look-see.

Phan sighed, hands on hips, shifting his gaze from Ivars to Cady and back again, noting the weapons each still clasped in cold fingers. "Takes two to tango."

"Looks like it, but if you want my two cents' worth, there's more to this than meets the eye." Jarvis said. "Better call downtown and get some techs out here."

Phan headed downstairs to the detectives' car. "Back in two shakes."

CHAPTER 24

Mr. Silly stood stock-still in Ramble's postage-stamp backyard. Poised just a few feet from the all-season porch, the dog held point, eyes riveted on a squirrel occupying an overhanging branch of a neighboring elm tree. The squirrel chattered and squawked at the resolute canine—to no avail. Mr. Silly remained stoic, on guard. The antics of dog and squirrel provided a carefree moment for the remaining students in Ramble's honors class, now holding impromptu meetings at his house. A week had passed since the bloody demise of Ivars Iverson and Norman Cady. Much had changed but not necessarily for the better. President Dingkudgel had called off the remainder of the semester, restricting students and faculty from the campus. Students evacuated the dorms. Professors could visit their offices only with special permission. The university all but ceased to operate.

The St. Paul police had yet to sort out a good reason for what they deemed to be a fatal shootout between Ivars and Cady. The TV and newspapers hustled gory details of the murders and banged a drum about the "Death of a University." President Dingkudgel had a full news conference scheduled for the next day. Gossip pouring out of the administrative offices heralded a permanent closing of the campus. The horrid publicity generated by the multiple murders on campus and the aftershocks to present and future enrollments made it unlikely the university could retain enough students to fill even a single dormitory. The hopes for new students enrolling dwindled to nothing. The adverse reaction of university alumni to the murders and to the drastic changes proposed by the Management by Vision initiative sank contributions to an all-time low. Corporate giving took a nosedive. Even the high muckety-muck of the Board of Regents, Bruce Haney, distanced himself from the university's president. Haney's public statements lamented the awful events of the fall semester, but eschewing the well-worn script of national political leaders, he did not issue statements about his and the Board of Regents' "full confidence" in the abilities and leadership of President Dingkudgel. Haney's refusal to play the game and toss off inspirational statements about the university and its leader increased the existing doo-doo to above the flood mark.

Dingkudgel persisted in his happy-happy, everything is hunky-dory, cloud cuckoo land behavior, wheeling and dealing for new online and classroom technology and issuing press releases about future graduate programs. He invited local sportswriters to a special luncheon to ask for opinions about candidates for the vacant football coaching job.

"Who will the guy coach?" Leo yelped as he read the news article.

Local colleges and universities jumped to the tawdry business of harvesting the best of Välkommen U's students and professors. Ramble spent hours going over his investments and TIAA-CREF accounts, attempting to foresee his future.

On the plus side, Ramble and several of his professor friends organized an ad hoc college for the students who remained in the Twin Cities. This shadow university proved a saving grace for all. The professors met once a week with the displaced students, and sometimes more often. These sessions ranged widely with discussion topics and readings.

Among Ramble's group of students, Melody, Josh, Amy, Ray, Jelani, and Elena lived in the Minneapolis-St. Paul area. Starry didn't return to her home in southern Minnesota. She hung out at a friend's apartment to be part of the class. Ramble sensed his students needed to be together, to do something other than obsessively gossip about the murders. He got them talking about their future plans and possible careers. Some harbored ideas about becoming college teachers. Ramble tried his best to answer their questions and give them advice, all the while striving to ignore his own misgivings.

"So exactly why did you decide to be a professor?" Melody sat curled up in one of the wicker chairs. She had mellowed out considerably outside the classroom and flourished within a more intimate group.

"Well, I guess I was born to it." Ramble explained that his parents had been academics—his father taught history at the university level and his mother had a part-time position teaching classics at a small college. "But I never planned to follow in their footsteps. Things sort of just happened."

The students looked disappointed at his explanation.

"OK. When it came time to think about my future, I liked the idea of no eight-to-five and being around young people. I have to admit the prospect of summers off had an appeal." Ramble struggled to recall exactly why he did follow his parents into college teaching. "I thought my teaching might make a difference. A better world. Things like that."

Ramble let it go. Given the perilous state of Välkommen University and the fact he might well be forced into an early retirement, Ramble found it difficult to conjure positive thoughts about being a college professor. To the students it probably seemed like a pretty good gig. Like most of the public, the kids didn't have a job description or a realistic, detailed list of hours, wages, roles, responsibilities, and potential disappointments.

Being a college professor could come packaged in several ways, most of which required some significant sacrifices and a lifetime of hard work for all but the chosen few. Being a successful college professor wasn't easy to define. The bar of success set by Ramble's father and his most admired professors always seemed quite clear, and for a variety of reasons, seemingly beyond reach. Publish books and articles, write successful grant proposals, and mentor a gang of bright graduate students. It didn't mean that other measures of success weren't useful and agreeable—maybe a younger generation of professors could find new ways of judging. But Ramble found it difficult to accept alternative versions of professorial attainment. How then would he sum up his career and go comfortably out the door with a smile on his face? A good question.

"Am I late for the Tupperware party?" Leo stood in the doorway between the porch and the kitchen, holding a beer in one hand and a cracker piled high with cheese spread in the other.

"Do you golf?" Melody walked over to Leo and led him to sit on one of the vacant chairs. Leo wore a pair of blue, green, and yellow madras Bermuda shorts and a white polo shirt. Somewhere in the historical section of his clothes closet, he'd found a white belt. His skinny legs were encased in a pair of knee-length black socks. All he lacked was a pair of tasseled loafers, Ramble thought. Leo assured Melody he did not play golf. His outfit merely indicated he was "at leisure."

"What is it you like best about being a college professor?" Josh asked Ramble, his eyes still fixed on Leo's ensemble.

"Let's do this instead," Ramble interrupted. "I'll tell you what I like best from students like you."

Leo took a sip of beer and regarded his friend without his usual playful expression. "Let's hear it, Professor."

"Best of all, I like students who are genuinely excited about what they're learning. After all these years, I can sort of tell if you'll be one of those after a few weeks of a semester. It's not just coming to class, making contributions to discussion, and things like that. I can tell when you're into it. Your eyes shine. You're eager to ask questions. You've got your own ideas about how things should be understood." Ramble smiled at the group. "You even drop by my office to discuss things with me, not just to angle for a better grade. That's when I know you're hooked. That's when I'm hooked."

Ramble recalled how he would wait until late in the afternoon hoping to catch his favorite undergraduate professor working in the library, perhaps welcoming a break and a short chat. By the time he hit grad school, Ramble would get so excited by a new article or something said in a readings seminar that not talking it over with his professors would eat at him. Every so often, one of his students would get the same fever.

"Enough of this professorial revelation." Leo blew across the top of his beer bottle for emphasis. "Inquiring minds want to know what you students think professors do all day. How about what makes Ramble and me a cut above the rest of our colleagues? Ah. Here's a good one. How would you build the perfect professor?"

The honors students took the bait Leo had cast. As they batted ideas back and forth, Leo would insert a playful observation. He led the group deep into debate about personal, professional, and pedagogical building blocks for the perfect professor. Ramble took the time to reflect about each of the students. He really knew little in depth about them as individuals, but during these get-togethers, personalities punched through easily, uncomplicated by a formal classroom setting. How much of a difference did that make in teaching and learning? At what depth of knowing did a teacher need to go with a student? Ramble doubted that most student surveys taken in a first class session did the job.

CHAPTER 25

"Professor, can we talk to you for a minute?" Starry and Josh waited by the door as the other students left the house. Starry twisted the strap of her backpack between her fingers. Josh nudged her, signaling she should forge ahead.

"We found out something really weird about Norman Cady."

Leo backtracked from the front entrance to hear what Starry had to say.

"Yeah. We're thinking about using him as the prototype for a character in a mystery," Josh said. "Remember, you told us to watch for things in the news and build characters and stories as if we were mystery writers. So with all that has happened, we thought Norman would be perfect, and we started a little background research on him."

"Did you know he worked at the East Oaks Country Club when he got out of prison last spring? It was part of a news story in the *Pioneer Press* about a halfway house in East St. Paul." Starry sat down on the edge of the sofa. She clasped her hands together on her knees, fingers working in a jittery pattern. "Josh's friend from high school caddies there. He told us Norman got a job fixing the golf carts."

Leo looked from Starry to Ramble and back again, his eyebrows drawn together in a puzzled arch. "So?"

"I think Starry and Josh have more to say here, Leo." Ramble had an inkling about which direction the story might take.

"We thought it was pretty odd that someone like Norman would get a job at a posh place like East Oaks Country Club," Josh said.

Leo nodded in agreement. "It's not like those East Oaks folks are a bunch of bleeding heart liberals."

Among all the private courses and country clubs in and around the Twin Cities area, East Oaks pretty much set the standard. A fantastic course with distinctive, memorable golf holes winding through a heavily wooded landscape and dramatic changes in elevation, East Oaks also treated golfers to a delightful harmony of what Minnesotans so prized—lush green fairways, majestic pines, and sky blue waters. Of course, this golfer's paradise came with a splendid clubhouse of prize-winning architectural design, an Olympic-size swimming pool bordered by a phalanx of water spas and poolside cabanas, and top-quality choices of dining and club rooms for members and their guests. Encircled by spectacular residences fetching prices well into the millions, an East Oaks membership came at a heavy financial price. Few but the most socially prominent elites could hope to wear the East Oaks logo on their custom-made polo shirts and blazers. Ramble suspected that for an ex-con lowlife like Norman Cady to find a slot on the payroll would take a powerful club member intervening on his behalf.

"One of the board members told the maintenance supervisor to hire Norman." Starry glanced at Josh for confirmation. "Josh's friend asked around for us. He said some of the other members were really jammed when they found out."

"Did your friend say who the board member was?" Ramble asked.

"No, but my friend saw Norman and that Bruce Haney guy talking behind the equipment shed a couple of times." Josh said.

Leo smiled at the young man. "You two did some superlative gumshoeing."

"You mean like those geeky detective movies from way back?" Josh asked.

"Ah . . . exactly."

Leo maneuvered his vintage 1970s VW bus south on Snelling Avenue. Not much traffic but enough for Leo to mobilize his full array of curses and gestures, shouting over a chorus of sounds emanating from the VW's engine. The Hippie Mobile, as Leo called his vehicle, also sported a rusted, pock-marked exterior with a distant baby blue and white paint job, set off by bumpers bent into shapes that looked like objects salvaged from some crank sculptor.

"I think we're on to something, Green Hornet." Leo glanced over at Ramble as he braked for a stoplight.

"What's that, Leo?"

"Well, for a start, why would a high-powered shady real estate and development mogul with an unhealthy interest in the future of our university consort with a violent offender and arrange employment for the little mobster's postprison release? A guy like that doesn't do anything without a dollar sign flashing."

"And?"

"One might speculate that a certain Mr. Bruce Haney, real estate developer extraordinaire, is masterminding a high-stakes game. Further, geeky gumshoe pal, he might have no compunction against using extreme means if it meant securing the prize."

"So what's the prize, Leo?" Ramble had an idea what it might be, but he waited for Leo's answer. Leo had a question for a question.

"If Välkommen U goes flooey, who gains?"

Ramble knew the answer. If Välkommen U self-destructed academically and financially—and the university seemed well on the way to that particular future—Inga Gadda would have to put her beloved institution on the block. Maybe she'd preserve the Nordic studies collection, but even the frozen foods heiress wouldn't have the cold cash to save the university. Was it a perfect setup for someone like Haney to make a multimillion-dollar real estate grab at bargain basement prices? Ramble was beginning to think so.

"If you see it the same way I do, Ramble, you know who gains."

Leo clunked by a semitrailer rig loaded with Schell's Beer, destined for the bars on West Seventh Street. "We'll have an upscale Gopher Valley rising like a Japanese horror movie rodent on the ruins of Välkommen University. Haney and his lap dog, Prexy Dingkudgel, will be three times as rich as they are now. Why is it the guys who have it always want more?"

If Leo's scenario made sense, the series of campus murders and Ding-kudgel's bizarre Management by Vision plan for the university gained a certain perverted logic. Ramble could appreciate Haney and Ding-kudgel's game plan. What better way to deep-six a university than to create conditions guaranteed to produce a ton of bad publicity that would drain the university's treasury, dry up contributions and grants, demoralize the faculty, and destroy enrollments? Were Haney and Dingkudgel capable of such a cold-hearted dangerous scheme? Maybe not Dingkudgel. But Haney? Yes indeed. The more Ramble thought about it, the less he doubted the scenario. But he needed to fill in the blanks. Fast.

The elderly club doorman recoiled from the sight of a smoking, oil-dripping clunker speeding up the curved flower-lined driveway leading to the East Oaks Country Club. This steadfast employee had protected that driveway and the massive entrance doors to the club for decades. Clad in an immaculate white uniform with brass buttons and spiffy epaulets, the doorman went on the offensive against the intruders. He rapped on the passenger side panel of the Hippie Mobile without a second thought about soiling his white gloves.

"Sir," he addressed Ramble. "Please inform your driver he cannot operate this . . . vehicle . . . in a restricted area without an official East Oaks Country Club permit clearly displayed on the right front bumper."

"Cool your jets, buddy," Leo warned the doorman from the driver's side. "This is no way to treat a VIP."

Ramble stepped out on the pavement, glaring at the doorman. "My driver will park our emergency vehicle if you will please direct him to the proper space."

The doorman retreated to his station near the clubhouse entrance doors, unsure of the developing situation.

"I'm with MSDRMEOM," Ramble informed his adversary.

Leo gave a low whistle. "Is it communicable?"

The doorman stared at Ramble. The acronym hung in the air between them. Ramble sighed. "That, my dear fellow, is the Minnesota State Department of Recreational Maintenance Equipment Oversight

Management." He figured a bogus state agency would suffice quite well in the situation. Minnesotans had a long acquaintance with state governmental inspection and oversight agencies covering a host of activities. Most of the state's citizenry would accept Ramble's fiction as legitimate government business. "Where do I find your maintenance facility?" he demanded.

Seeking a quick and satisfactory solution to the immediate problem of a ghastly inappropriate vehicle littering the club driveway and its driver garbed in an golf outfit not seen at East Oaks in many a year, the doorman gave directions to the employee parking lot adjacent to the maintenance shed. Leo fired up the Hippie Mobile and headed to the parking lot, leaving the doorman batting away a cloud of exhaust smoke.

The sole employee in the maintenance shed informed Ramble that Josh's friend had long since left the premises for the day. Ramble and Leo walked around the building to the back door. There they could glimpse part of the tenth fairway. Halfway down a short dogleg par four, a lone cart with two golfers angled across the lush green fairway to a ball resting at the top of a hill. In the stillness of the evening, Ramble could make out the sounds of a furious argument between the two golfers. The driver seemed to be doing most of the shouting.

Leo shielded his eyes against the setting sun. "Isn't that our dear friends, Messrs. Haney and Dingkudgel? A little late in the day to be heading off on the back nine, isn't it?"

"Come on, Leo." Ramble sprinted for a line of golf carts parked for recharging alongside the maintenance shed. "I've got a bad feeling."

"Floor it." Leo commanded, watching the club doorman running toward them and waving for their attention. Ramble pointed the cart down the wood-chip path bordering the tenth fairway.

As Ramble and Leo approached the tip of the dogleg just before the cart path plunged downhill into a sharp S curve, they caught a glimpse of Haney and Dingkudgel standing on the green. The two men seemed to be involved in a pushing and shoving match, but a tunnel of soaring pines engulfed the speeding golf cart, cutting off Ramble's view of the quarrel.

"*Yeeeooow.*" Leo went flying out of the golf cart as Ramble yanked the steering wheel right then left to navigate the S curve. The last thing Ramble saw was a pair of skinny legs swathed in black knee socks up-ended behind an evergreen bush beside the cart path.

"Keep going, Ramble," came the call from Leo. "I'll catch up."

In a short but agonizing couple of minutes of racing, Ramble emerged from the line of trees and parked the golf cart at greenside. President Dingkudgel lay on the closely mowed surface, blood leaking from a nasty gash across his temple; his left foot, shod in a two-tone baby blue and white golf shoe, quivered spasmodically.

"He lied to me," moaned the stricken president as Ramble sprinted toward him. Tears streamed down Dingkudgel's cheeks. "I can't be-lieve he'd do such horrible things."

Dingkudgel rocked back and forth, moaning pitifully, tears stream-ing down his face. "He said I'd gone soft on him . . . that I couldn't take the heat."

Ramble helped the crestfallen administrator to his feet, despite an urge to stuff the spineless clown face first into a nearby sand trap.

CHAPTER 26

A Week Later

"Damn fool. He couldn't talk fast enough." Detective Jarvis eased back into the chocolate brown leather couch in the president's office suite. "Squawked like a parrot."

"Snitched on his buddy like a guy with his pants on fire." Phan sat perched on a portable massage table ex-President Dingkudgel had used for his daily rubdown. "Kept saying Haney pulled a fast one on him."

The two detectives, Leo, Angela, and Ramble sat in the spacious executive office a few weeks after the incident at East Oaks Country Club. They were mulling over the capture and arrest of Bruce Haney who had traded in his three-piece suit for something not quite so fashionable and bright glaring orange in color. Haney awaited a preliminary hearing on murder charges. Dingkudgel shared the same address and in-house fashion consultant.

"I wish I'd been there to see it, Professor Ramble," said Jarvis. "Sounds like you had fun."

Ramble nodded in agreement. "More exciting than an end-of-the-year department meeting."

After discovering a semiconscious totally hysterical Dingkudgel on the 10th green, Ramble had yelled back up the fairway at Leo to take

care of the injured university president. Leo came limping out of the
trees and brush where he'd landed, looking like a freaked-out Chester
on a vintage TV episode of *Gunsmoke.*

Ramble jumped back into his cart and took off after a fleeing Haney
who could be glimpsed piloting his cart across the bridge leading to
the 16th hole. After a rousing chase across tees and fairways, including
an unfortunate mishap with a lone golfer exiting a Porta-Potty, Ramble
finally caught up with Haney. The front wheels of the bedraggled
man's golf cart sat half in the mud and muck of a small algae-laden
pond. Haney eschewed an attempt at pushing his cart back on dry land
and scrambled back to the fairway, green muck covering his legs to the
knees. He posed in a weird defensive posture, snarling, apparently
ready to fight.

Ramble vaulted out of the golf cart and stood a couple of yards from
the desperate fugitive. "Kung fu, Brucie."

Haney made a sound like an angry grackle, leaped forward and
kicked a gunk-caked foot out. Ramble brushed the kick aside and
caught Haney with a basic right uppercut to the chin.

"So much for secret fighting strategies of the ancient Chinese."
Ramble grabbed a blubbering Haney by his belt and yanked him up
from the grass. He stood his captive up like a golf bag in the back of
the cart. Using the straps meant to secure the golf bags, Ramble
cinched Haney securely around the waist. For good measure, Ramble
grabbed several of Haney's clubs and wedged them in their owner's
bonds. Haney was in no shape to escape and endured the long ride
back to the clubhouse in silence.

"That was the saddest-looking golf bag I've ever seen." Leo sat behind Dingkudgel's desk, his feet up on a nearby file drawer, hands
clasped behind his head. "Wish I'd had a camera."

"There were plenty of TV reporters there by that time, Professor,"
Phan said. "You can probably get a videotape."

"The prosecutor will have a field day with the news reports." Jarvis
shook his head in wonder. "The two of them yelling at each other, and
Dingkudgel accusing Haney of breach of verbal contract."

At that particular moment, as Ramble recalled, several prominent
defense attorneys stumbled out of the 19th Hole Cocktail Cabana

shouting things like "objection," "take the fifth," and "no olives in mine." In no time, the two most agile, least-gassed of the barroom barristers had established legal representation for the two potential clients but not soon enough to quiet Dingkudgel from lamenting his "fall from righteousness" and "descent into a slough of temptation and sinfulness." All the while, a furious Haney screamed at his coconspirator to "stop acting like a Sunday morning televangelist" and "shut the hell up."

"They almost pulled it off." Phan gathered up the microrecording devices he'd used earlier for the formal interview. "Ivars Iverson and Norman Cady were doing the dirty work—thinking they would have a life on Easy Street. We would have likely pulled the plug on our investigation after Haney staged the double murder." Phan shrugged. "If it weren't for you two professors and those students in your class, we'd have never suspected more than what was in front of our noses."

"Thanks, Detectives," Ramble said. "I think you're shortchanging yourselves a bit."

"All's well that ends well." Leo said.

"All over but the shouting." Ramble added, hoping to jump-start the detectives' usual wisecracking routine.

Jarvis and Phan glanced at each other, apparently not catching on. "Thanks for your help. I'm sure we'll be back in touch soon," Jarvis said, backing out the door.

Phan hesitated. He smiled at Leo. "By the way, Professor DaVita, congratulations. Sounds like you have a ton of work in front of you."

"Thank you, Detective." Leo removed his reading glasses and examined the lenses for any specks and smudges. He fiddled with the fancy laptop computer on Dingkudgel's desk, a sparkle in his eyes. "It's nothing I can't handle."

Subsequent to the arrests and rapid indictments of President Dingkudgel and Bruce Haney, the aging heiress, Inga Gadda, leaped to the fore to help put the crumbled pieces of her beloved university back together. She seemed to have found new energy, a new purpose in the midst of tragic circumstances. In an initial bold move, she summoned Leo from retirement, appointing him interim president of Välkommen U. The new appointee assured the Twin Cities' press he was "still alive,

and in partial possession of his faculties—all I have ever observed necessary for the majority of college presidents." The press immediately
adopted Leo and hounded him about town. As the new university
leader explained it: "I am a moving, grooving quote machine."

In another unexpected, dynamic maneuver, Inga reassumed the
reins at Gadda Swedish Frozen Foods, and within a day introduced a
completely new item on the list of products—something she'd been
working on in her kitchen for a decade. News of the Välkommen Pölsa
Health Bar—a taste-pleasing mix of walleye and small mouth bass
parts, beef intestines, fiber of potato, pure North Woods water, natural
grains, and spices ("but not too spicy")—made the front pages in Minneapolis and St. Paul. Preproduction orders poured in for the new ethnic health treat. Grocers cleared whole bins to shelve it. Fishermen
throughout the state pleaded for an early release. Stock in Gadda Swedish Frozen Foods skyrocketed, and Inga held a press conference to announce that 40% of expected profits would be donated to the
university.

Leo's appointment came as quite a shock to the university community, of course, but it made perfect sense to his patroness. More than
any other individual, Leo possessed a splendid institutional memory.
Inga Gadda had it in mind to create an ideal, small liberal arts community of students and scholars fit for the demands of the twenty-first
century. Acting on that vision, Leo took the helm and within a matter
of days had stirred up considerable excitement and support for what
became known as the the Välkommen University Game Plan. Alumni
rallied to their alma mater with pledges of resources, volunteerism, and
financial support. Leo further excited local and national interest by
establishing a Web site to brainstorm aspects of a new Välkommen
University.

"If you could create a liberal arts university best fit to meet the
demands of the twenty-first century, what would that institution be?"
The question stirred up debate and submissions from throughout the
ranks of American higher education and beyond. Each day, Leo, Ramble, and Angela gathered in the president's conference room to read
and discuss the results.

"It's amazing what we've received on the Web site," Leo exulted. "I'll bet there are more than a thousand responses and suggestions in just three days." He adjusted the knot on his blazing red tie. He'd paired his new cravat with a blue blazer jacket and gray slacks, all purchased under Angela's supervision. "I feel like a salesman at some fancy corporate menswear shop," Leo said, obviously enjoying his transition from professor emeritus to college president. He had some lunchtime schmoozing to do with Inga Gadda and executives from one of the local foundations.

"You and Inga are getting pretty tight, aren't you?" Ramble teased his friend. "Next thing we'll know is that you two are an item."

Leo brushed off crumbs from a glazed donut sticking to the lapel of his blazer. He leaned back in his leather chair and regarded Ramble with a smug look. "Inga is a very pleasing benefit of my new executive status."

Ramble smiled at Angela, expecting her to join him in razzing Välkommen U's new president. But she frowned, her eyes clouding with worry.

"What's up?" Ramble asked.

"I was just thinking. If Leo and Inga ever got married . . . she'd be Inga Gadda Da—"

Leo cut off Angela's speculation with a stern expression and warned, "That'll be quite enough, the both of you."

DEADLY PROFESSORS

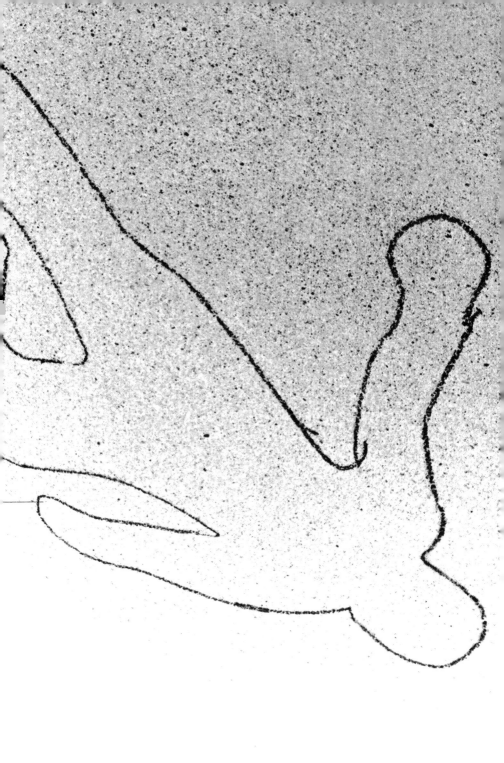

DEADLY PROFESSORS

Workshop Discussion Questions and
Other Faculty Development Activities

Thomas B. Jones

STERLING, VIRGINIA

Published by Stylus Publishing, LLC
22883 Quicksilver Drive
Sterling, Virginia 20166–2102

Library of Congress Cataloging-in-Publication-Data
Jones, Thomas B., 1942-
  Deadly professors : workshop discussion questions
and other faculty development activities / Thomas B.
Jones.—1st ed.
      p.   cm.
  Includes bibliographical references and index.
  ISBN 978–1-57922–449–3 (cloth : alk. paper)
  ISBN 978–1-57922–450–9 (pbk. : alk. paper)
  1. College personnel management.   2. Teacher-
administrator relationships.   3. Teachers' workshops.
I. Title.
LB2331.66.J64   2010
378.1'1—dc22   2009050711

13-digit ISBN: 978–1-57922–449–3 (cloth)
13-digit ISBN: 978–1-57922–450–9 (paper)

Printed in the United States of America

All first editions printed on acid free paper
that meets the American National Standards Institute
Z39–48 Standard.

Bulk Purchases

Quantity discounts are available for use in
workshops and for staff development.
Call 1–800–232–0223

First Edition, 2010

10   9   8   7   6   5   4   3   2   1

Contents

LIVELY DISCUSSIONS ABOUT
DEADLY PROFESSORS

Those who have read the chapters in *Deadly Professors* probably will not have to depend on this section of the book to initiate workshop discussions and other faculty development activities. The great majority of chapters and the book as a whole contain issues, dilemmas, and everyday situations familiar to those involved in higher education. Conversations and worthwhile discussions among individuals from a variety of disciplines and academic backgrounds will be easy enough to fashion, especially if those involved will share their unique expertise, experience, and perspectives (rarely have I found college professors to be shrinking violets in this regard). But on the off chance that a starting point might be necessary, I have put together some general discussion questions and a few supplemental materials.

In writing the book I found a great deal of useful research and reading covering most of the topics included in the action of the mystery story. The usual suspects, such as *The Chronicle of Higher Education, Change Magazine, The National Teaching and Learning Forum, The Teaching Professor, The Journal on Excellence in College Teaching,* and *College Teaching* are recommended, as are the books and journals from

publishers like Stylus, Jossey-Bass, and Anker Press. Pointing a browser to the higher education Web sites (for example, InsideHigherEd, MountainRise, Merlot, and Innovate) will provide a variety of information about trends and issues in teaching and learning, higher education, distance learning, and technology. Dalhousie University's Office of Instructional Development and Technology supplies a nice listing of university and college sites (across the globe) devoted to teaching and faculty development (http://learningandteaching.dal.ca/ids.html).

Issues for Discussion

Chapter 2—Midcareer and senior faculty issues and problems; professors making a difference?

Chapter 3—Faculty roles and responsibilities; academic leadership for departments; faculty decision making. I have borrowed some terms and ideas for this chapter from John F. Wergin's study, *Departments That Work: Building and Sustaining Cultures of Excellence in Academic Programs* (Bolton, MA: Anker, 2003). Michael Fischer's, "Defending Collegiality," *Inside Higher Education* (April 30, 2009) available at http://www.insidehighereducation.com proved most helpful on the pros and cons of collegiality.

Chapter 4—Today's college students; students and technology; the on-campus educational experience.

Chapter 5—Issues of liberal education and liberal learning (critics, claims, definitions, real-world connections, etc.).

Chapter 6—The first class session; classroom incivility. Early chapters of Patrick Allitt's book *I'm the Teacher, You're the Student* (Philadelphia: University of Pennsylvania Press, 2005) provided ideas and incidents for imagining Professor Ramble and his students in their first class session. However one looks at it, the first class session is of prime importance, and as Allitt and others make clear, it can make or break a semester for students and their professors.

Chapter 8—African American Studies and faculty hiring; diversity and conflict; racial microaggressions; American faculty (problems and pressures). My reading in the following sources is reflected in this chapter: Lois Benjamin, *Black Women in Academy* (Tallahassee: University Press of Florida, 1997), Gail L. Thompson and Angela C. Louque, *Exposing the "Culture of Arrogance" in the Academy* (Sterling, VA: Stylus, 2005), Noliwe Rooks, *White Money/Black Power: The History of African American Studies and the Crisis in Higher Education* (Boston: Beacon Press, 2006), and Gargi Roysircar-Sodowsky, "Getting Along with Colleagues: A Cultural Perspective," in R.

McLaren Sawyer, Keith W. Pritchard, Karl D. Hostetler, eds., *The Art and Politics of College Teaching: A Practical Guide for the Beginning Professor* (New York: Peter Lang, 2004) provided ideas for this chapter. Two articles in a special issue of the *Chronicle of Higher Education, Diversity* (September 28, 2007) by Jennifer Delton, "Why Diversity for Diversity's Sake Won't Work" and Richard A. Tapia's "True Diversity Doesn't Come From Abroad" were useful. On racial microaggressions, see Derald Wing Sue and others, "Racial Microaggressions in Everyday Life: Implications for Clinical Practice," *American Psychologist* (May–June 2007), pp. 271–286, and Sue, Kevin L. Nadal, and others, "Racial Microaggressions Against Black Americans: Implications for Counseling," *Journal of Counseling & Development* (Summer 2008), pp. 330–338. Another perspective is William A. Smith, Walter R. Allen, and Lynette L. Danley, " 'Assume the Position . . . You Fit the Description': Psychosocial Experiences and Racial Battlefield Fatigue Among African Male College Students," *American Behavioral Scientist* (December 2007) 5(4), pp. 551–578.

Chapter 10—Teaching innovation and opportunity.

Chapter 11—Senior professors; academic retirement. Peter Seldon makes a number of sensible suggestions about "rejuvenating 'tired' professors" in *Chronicle of Higher Education*, "Point of View," (March 7, 2008), A26.

Chapters 12 and 13—Technology and learning; technology, teaching, and faculty development; the lecture. Mary Burgan, former general secretary of the American Association of University Professors (AAUP), had much to say about the value of the lecture in a *Change Magazine* article (November–December, 2006, pp. 30–34). That article and the exchanges it occasioned are reflected to some extent in this chapter.

Chapter 15—Classroom indoctrination and balance; academic freedom; issues about ratemyprofessors.com, YouTube, and so on. A tour of Web sites from YouTube to ratemyprofessors.com to studentsforacademicfreedom.com would be instructive for workshop discussions. For the ongoing argument about liberal bias in academe and academic freedom, take a sample from David Horowitz at

frontpagemag.com versus Michael Berube, *What's Liberal About the Liberal Arts: Classroom Politics and "Bias" in Higher Education* (New York: Norton, 2006). "Freedom in the Classroom" from AAUP is available from www.aaup.org/AAUP/comm/rep/A/class.htm. *Indoctrinate U* is a film produced by critics of liberal bias and lack of balance in teaching (http://indoctrinate-u.com/pages/welcome.html). Scott Jaschik's article, "Reframing the Debate About What Professors Say" and Michael Berube's "Freedom to Teach" *InsideHigherEducation.com* (September 11, 2007) are worth reading about the AAUP statement and Horowitz's reaction.

Chapter 17—Professors as role models? academic blogging.

Chapters 19 and 20—Multiculturalism and undergraduates; delicate situations in the classroom.

Chapter 20 takes off from an interesting article by Robert S. Levine ("Reconsideration: Teaching in the Multiracial Classroom: Reconsidering Melville's *Benito Cereno*," *MELUS*, *19*(1), Varieties of Ethnic Criticism (Spring, 1994), 111–120, and chapters from David Denby's *Great Books: My Adventures with Homer, Rousseau, Woolf and other Indestructible Writers of the Western World* (New York: Simon & Schuster, 1996).

Chapter 21—Online distance learning; adjunct faculty; lifelong learning.

Chapter 22—Sports and undergraduate education.

Chapter 24—A successful academic career; the perfect professor; knowing students.

Chapter 26—The ideal liberal arts college for the 21st century.

DISCUSSION QUESTIONS

Suggestion: For most of the following chapters, an interesting prework-shop or postworkshop activity might be organized based on the following question: How would you rewrite the chapter to reflect your individual, departmental, or institutional setting?

Chapter 2

1. What sorts of issues, difficulties, changes, and opportunities should professors expect as they enter the middle and later years of their academic careers? What are the most important interests and concerns of senior faculty? How can faculty recognize when they are "stuck" and losing their passion and commitment for academic life?

2. What conflicts and differences might be expected between older professors and younger faculty? What are possible avenues of cooperation and growth? What kinds of faculty development programs might help deal with conflicts and open new opportunities?

3. What types of faculty development activities would be most useful for the concerns and problems of senior professors? Does your institution have programs or formative post-tenure reviews for senior professors' continued professional development? What about faculty development approaches to expand or create new roles and responsibilities for senior professors? Learning communities?

4. How can professors "make a difference" in their career roles as teachers and faculty members? What evidence is available to measure impacts on students, colleagues, institutions, and communities?

5. Jack Ramble complains, "I'm facing my declining years of teaching without much confidence, little idealism, and a bag full of useless humor, metaphors, and stories." What advice would you offer Ramble?

Chapter 3

1. What are the unique aspects of faculty roles that President Ding-kudgel seems unable to recognize?

2. How would you describe faculty within a department working together at their best? What are the necessary conditions and support for faculty in an academic department or program unit to work together at the highest levels of cooperation and efficiency?

3. How would you define "academic leadership" for a department? What would you suggest to department chairs like Jack Ramble to best work with faculty and motivate them to create unity and a quality program? What specific steps could Ramble take as a department chair to promote collegiality?

4. AAUP stands against any collegiality criteria connected to evaluation of faculty. In a 1993 statement the AAUP argues:

> In the heat of important decisions regarding promotion or tenure, as well as other matters involving such traditional areas of faculty responsibility as curriculum or academic hiring, collegiality may be confused with the expectation that a faculty member display "enthusiasm" or "dedication," "evince" a constructive attitude that will "foster harmony," or display an excessive deference to administrative or faculty decisions where these may require reasoned discussion. Such expectations are flatly contradictory to elementary principles of academic freedom, which protect a faculty member's right to dissent from the judgments of colleagues and administrations.

Does the AAUP have a good case on this issue?

5. Jack Ramble expresses the idea that in theory faculty ought to be great at academic self-government and decision making (and should be contributing, responsible members of a group). Do you agree? What are the understandings, skills, and characteristics of faculty that might support the theory? What gets in the way of matching theory and reality?

6. Of course, faculty are not exactly employees of a business corporation. But in some ways colleges and universities are like corporations. What might someone in management or employed in a

corporate setting wonder about faculty and their responses to change initiatives, leadership, and management decisions?

7. As a faculty member, what might you include on a list of professional commitments to your department colleagues? To students? To administrators and staff? (For example: Faculty will provide timely responses to students' assignments, return communications promptly, and make appropriate advising referrals.) What would you suggest as items for a list of commitments from students to the faculty? (For example: Students will think and act on their education in a mature and responsible manner in the classroom and in interactions with faculty, staff, and fellow students.)

8. What are the major stumbling blocks and frustrations faculty and administrators face in terms of decision making? What are the possible solutions?

9. What would you suggest to the Välkommen U English department about finding its place in a larger university mission and best contributing faculty's talents and energies to that ideal? What would be on your list of suggestions for your own department or program in this regard?

Chapter 4

1. What have you noticed about your students in terms of learning styles, values, opinions, and so on that match the latest national surveys and research about a new generation of undergraduates? What does your institution offer you in terms of useful information and studies about changes in students' characteristics? What sorts of changes in your teaching, advising, and work with these new students might be necessary?

2. Do class schedules and academic calendars reflect faculty priorities or student needs at your institution? What changes can you suggest that would promote better teaching and learning, better use of faculty time, and so on?

3. Should each university and college strive to offer a unique educational experience? Is this still possible in 21st-century higher education? How does an institution preserve its unique educational experience in face of significant changes in American culture, learning technologies, and such?

4. Is Professor Ramble unduly harsh and suspicious in his assessment of new learning and information technologies? In your teaching and discipline, does it matter if students read assignments from available technologies as opposed to traditional print sources?

5. News columnist J. Peder Zane suggests that traditional-age students on today's college campuses lack curiosity and care little about what they don't know. Do you agree? What can professors do to confront this problem in their classes? (see J. Peder Zane, "Lack of Curiosity Is Curious" *Charlotte News and Observer*, November 6, 2005, C15.)

6. What do you think are the primary skills, understandings, and attitudes expected of students once they move into professions and careers? How much of a gap is there, in your opinion, between the skills, abilities, and attitudes students bring to campus and what is then expected of them in the postundergraduate professional world? What do you and others on your campus do to discuss and address this gap? What more could be attempted throughout the campus and in your own teaching and advising?

Chapter 5

1. What would you identify as typical objections and criticisms directed against liberal education by students and their parents? How would you respond to these objections and criticisms based on your institution's guidelines and requirements?
2. In general, do you agree there is a gap between claims made throughout higher education for the value of a liberal education and what is delivered? What would you identify as possible causes for this gap? What is the situation on your campus?
3. In terms of your college or university, how would you define a general education? A liberal education? How would you explain your institution's definitions and approach to students and parents?
4. What connections do you see between liberal education and success in a career or profession?
5. What are the characteristics, skills, and values most esteemed in the careers your institution's undergraduate students will most likely pursue upon graduation? How does your required curriculum help build those characteristics, skills, and values?
6. Mr. Haney asks, "Beyond the rationale and, excuse me, the rhetoric about the value of the liberal arts, what's taking place in the courses and how they are taught seems pretty important. What proof have we that good things occur? Are the various departments engaged in these required courses working together for a final product?" As a representative for your department or academic area, how would you respond?

Chapter 6

1. Why is the first class session so important to a successful semester of teaching?
2. What would you tell Ramble he has done well as a teacher in this first class session; for example, in overall approach, teaching, interactions with students?
3. What are the mistakes and misjudgments in Ramble's approach to his first class in terms of planning and teaching?
4. What should Ramble know, reconsider, and revise before the next time he teaches a first class session for his course?
5. What other strategies might Ramble consider in terms of damage control for the next class meeting?
6. Before a first class, what should you have done to prepare—not just materials, syllabus, readings, teaching strategies, and such, but in terms of research and thinking about the students you'll teach?
7. Think about how you approach and handle your first class. What are your goals for it? How do you teach it? What advice can you offer to your colleagues? What have you learned, and how might you revise the first class?
8. Do some of the incidents in this first session fit your definition of classroom incivility? Where does the fault lie for any examples you identify as classroom incivility? What are the possible causes and fixes? Is there any best approach professors can use to deal with classroom incivility in the first class session or first week of a semester?
9. A professor at Syracuse University (as reported in *Inside Higher Ed*, http://www.insidehighered.com/news/2008/04/02/texting) made the decision to walk out of his large lecture classes when students sent text messages or read a newspaper in class. The professor saw it this way: "Everyone has to understand that respect is a two-way street. . . . My experience has been that confronting students directly and asking them to stop has virtually no effect. I walk out to underscore the importance of what this means to me." Do you agree with this professor's decision and reasoning? What other alternatives might be available? A student had this reaction to the

professor's decision: "We students are the customer, the ones who make the the choice every day to pay attention or not." The student goes on to tell what a large sum of money he pays for tuition and states that his professor "gets paid whether his students text in class or not." The students asks, "Does he think this is the first time this has happened on any college campus? Had he acted like 100 percent of the other college professors in this country, he would have shrugged it off and continued his lecture." What would be your response to this student?

Chapter 8

1. What negative recruiting and retention factors do African American and other faculty from diverse ethnic backgrounds face on your campus?

2. How might perceptions of an African American Studies program (or program areas similar to it, e.g., Native American, Chicano/a, Asian) and its role within a college or university differ among administrators, program faculty, the faculty at large, students, and community? What problems and issues might arise from these differing perceptions?

3. What are some of the professional and personal difficulties faced by faculty with appointments in African American studies (and programs similar to it) in their work with administration, other faculty, students, and the community? Should these faculty members expect to have a special role on campus? How would that special role be defined on your campus?

4. Are Sam's fears about the future of African American studies and its use for affirmative action/student recruitment goals reasonable? What are the resulting negative effects and frustrations for African American faculty and students? How might other groups and constituencies on a campus be affected?

5. How do you understand and define diversity and affirmative action in your setting? Is Ramble right in his suspicion that diversity might shortchange the representation and future of American minority groups whose difficult position within American society remains so visible?

6. How would you rate the quality of this interview? What is troubling about its structure? In interviewing candidates for faculty positions, what should faculty strive for in portraying their institution, department, and location as a place to work? What would be the ideal structure and approach of a committee engaged in interviewing Nadine for a position on the faculty? What sorts of preinterview actions should such a committee be prepared to tackle?

7. What are examples of unintended racial microaggressions that might occur in an academic/campus setting (classroom, advising,

campus activities, faculty interactions with other faculty, etc.)? What sorts of reactions and strategies might faculty adopt for classroom and advising instances of racial microaggression? What might be some of the emotional, psychological, and physical signs of a student's "racial battle fatigue" resulting from racial microaggressions? If racial microaggressions can be unintended, why must they be seen as a cause for concern? What is the baseline for identifying an unintended gesture or remark as being a racial microaggression? What are the pros and cons of applying the racial microaggression concept in academic life?

8. Nadine mentions several problems and pressures faced by African American faculty in new settings, such as inadequate mentoring systems, geographic and social isolation, student racism in the classroom (especially in those taught by African American women), and a difficult expectation for such faculty to fit in with the dominant culture. How would you describe your campus environment? What improvements and changes should be discussed?

Chapter 10

1. How would you handle a situation such as the one Ramble faces with the honors students? What opportunities do you see in this situation for a teacher? What techniques and strategies would you use in this first class session?
2. What are the pros and cons of allowing students to chart the direction of a course or section within a course? Would you allow students this freedom? Why or why not?
3. What are some of the themes you would suggest for a class of top students in your discipline or program area? What sorts of themes do you think students would suggest? What themes and topics for a course do you think students would deem most interesting and relevant?

Chapter 11

1. Is there a comprehensive program of preretirement planning for continued, informal service at your institution? What are some career options for retired professors? Does your institution or department/program area consider the possibilities of using retired professors for part-time teaching, mentoring, advising, and so on?
2. Christopher Phelps suggests that "Retirement is a hiring issue. Retirement is central to the renewal of the American university." Agree or disagree? (see Christopher Phelps, "We Need to See Retirement as a Hiring Issue [*Chronicle Review*, April 25, 2010], A.)
3. Like most men and women in any career facing retirement, how can individuals in academic life know when it is time for retirement? What steps should soon-to-retire professors take to prepare for leaving full-time positions?
4. What are some of the most prominent issues and difficulties facing senior professors who are nearing retirement? What unique understandings and abilities do senior faculty possess that could be used for positive change in a department, university structure, and such?
5. Is being an academic professor what Leo says it is: "It's sure as hell different from any occupation I can think of"? In regard to the issue of retirement and other aspects of academic careers (leadership, decision making, etc.), what are the similarities and differences between faculty members and individuals in other professions and career settings?
6. What are some of the most prominent issues and difficulties facing senior professors who are nearing retirement? What, if any, are the obligations of senior professors to younger colleagues? What essential knowledge and wisdom might senior professors bequeath to younger colleagues?

Chapters 12 and 13

1. How have the Internet and other technologies influenced and changed learning for students at the college level?
2. What training and orientation is now necessary for students to use technology successfully for learning? What do their teachers need to know? What faculty development activities can be used most successfully to help faculty learn about and use technology? What is the library's role?
3. How might technology enhance your teaching? How could you revise your courses to employ technology with purpose and success for student learning? Is support for technology a problem on your campus? What do you need in terms of support? What can be done to bring about a better working relationship?
4. What are the pros and cons of the lecture strategy? Is there a difference among the disciplines concerning the lecture and its usefulness as a teaching-learning strategy?
5. How would you respond to Ramble's statement about technology: "Students didn't need more of what they had taken to the extreme. They needed to talk with people who like to discuss important ideas. Talking, listening, reading, writing, reflecting—there was a good prescription for active, substantial learning. Students didn't need extra doses of—what was it? Facebook. They needed real books with covers and pages. Somewhere he'd read another good prescription: Make sure your students put in some hard work to develop the intellectual stamina and the ability to ask questions that don't lead to easy answers. He didn't think messing around all the time with technology could accomplish that."
6. What do you see as the dangers of technology for your classroom learning approaches and strategies? What are the benefits?
7. Is technology best used to save valuable class time for active learning strategies as opposed to lecture, to promote student-to-student and teacher-to-student interactions? If so, how would you employ technology in one of your courses to give students the necessary

background and information for classroom discussions and active learning? Which technologies would you use?

8. How could you use technology to keep students thinking and working on course issues and problems outside your classroom?

Chapter 15

1. Should professors pay any attention to Web sites popular with students, such as MySpace, YouTube, and ratemyprofessors.com? How might such Web sites be used for student learning?
2. Critics of liberal political bias in undergraduate education have stepped up attacks on college and university professors in recent years. These critics advocate an "academic bill of rights" designed to balance the political perspectives students encounter in their courses (professors, readings, etc.) and in campus life. If there is lack of balanced perspectives and indoctrination of students by liberal professors, is it a good idea, a necessity, to legislate an academic bill of rights at the campus or state level? How does (might) this controversy affect your teaching and your campus?
3. What do recent studies report about on-campus political activism and left-wing political indoctrination of students? Is the problem, as one researcher suggests, too little focus on political issues and the political process rather than too much?
4. What exactly is "academic freedom?" How can you define it with reference to your teaching? What are some of the actions professors might take in the classroom that go beyond what you define as academic freedom?
5. Does academic freedom apply only in the classroom? Does it extend to other campus activities? Does it extend beyond professors to administrators and staff?
6. One observer (Stanley Fish, "Conspiracy Theories 101," *New York Times,* July 23, 2006, http://www.nytimes.com/2006/07/23/opin ion/23fish.html) of the debate about bias and academic freedom has argued, "Any idea can be brought into a classroom if the point is to inquire into its structure, history, influence and so forth. But no idea belongs in the classroom if the point of introducing it is to recruit your students for the political agenda it may be thought to imply." How does this statement fit for you as a guideline?
7. Where do you stand in regard to this observation: "The sensible professor nowadays takes it for granted that everything he or she says in the classroom can be—and very likely is being—recorded

(lots of mobile telephones now have this capability). Whether this subsequently becomes fodder for political blogs, ratemyprofessors .com or just for a student's suitemates shouldn't make any difference" (comment sent to the *Chronicle of Higher Education* from Gustave, September 12, 2007).

8. What are some controversial topics and ideas contained in your courses that could lead to situations similar to that faced by Nadine in this chapter? How would you approach and handle such instances? What advice and general principles would you share with a new faculty member? What are the thoughts and actions of a responsible teacher whose course subjects are likely to involve controversy and misunderstandings? What might be the learning opportunities available in classrooms experiencing intense controversy and heightened misunderstandings among students and between students and their teacher?

Chapter 17

1. If professors are indeed role models, how does one go about being one inside and outside the classroom? What are the potential problems of professors attempting to be role models?

2. Blogging is now it seems an accepted and growing aspect of academic life. What possibilities do you see in this form for substantive, scholarly dialogue and contribution? Are some fields and disciplines more likely to see positive uses for the blog? Any risks for faculty engaged in blogging? Should faculty be encouraged to engage in blogging? Is the use of pseudonyms in academic blogging appropriate?

Chapters 19 and 20

1. What are the positive and negative aspects of multiculturalism in the classroom for students? For professors? Do the stakes and issues of multiculturalism differ significantly depending on who is involved as a student or a professor? What prepares and qualifies someone to introduce and discuss issues of multiculturalism objectively with students?

2. What are some of the misperceptions, stereotypes, and troublesome realities students like Jelani might have to face in higher education? In addition to the vast generational difference between Ramble and Jelani, what other barriers might separate this professor and his student?

3. How would you advise Ramble on handling the troubling, delicate situation his class experienced? What could he and his students do to repair the damage? How could they learn from the incident? How might incidents such as this class experienced be prevented? What specifically could Ramble do to better monitor the issues of diversity in his classroom?

4. What do you assume most of your students think about multiculturalism? How do you respond to their views and opinions about multiculturalism? What sort of overall discussion of multiculturalism might faculty pursue with one another? With students?

5. In chapter 20 one of Ramble's students complains, "I go from class to class, and I can't seem to put everything I hear into something that makes sense for me." She goes on to say, "Sometimes I feel like I'm being forced to accept some recipe. It doesn't seem much different from memorizing periodic elements in chemistry." How would you respond to a student who raised these concerns?

Chapter 21

1. A number of colleges and universities have adopted the electronic classroom, televised instruction, and online distance learning programs. The arguments for and against this type of learning are many. What are the reasons why a college or university should consider the development of online programs? What are some of the main arguments in favor of offering online courses? What dangers and inequalities can result for students and professors from such learning systems?

2. If online programs flourish and grow successful, at what point will an institution need to reconsider basic mission and structure? What pressures, if any, would a successful online learning program exert on the mission and curriculum of a traditional campus environment?

3. Haney makes the argument that if university students "are to be successful in the world of work and in twenty-first-century society [they] must have solid experience as independent learners. They must conduct independent research. They must master the intricacies of a booming Internet marketplace of knowledge, ideas, and communication. Online study is the answer." What is your response?

4. The role of adjunct faculty has increased substantially in higher education. What are some of the problems and issues faced by adjunct faculty? What are the positive and negative effects of increased use of adjunct faculty for a college or university (e.g., for students, full-time faculty, administration, curriculum, etc.)? What do you see as fair roles, responsibilities, and benefits for adjunct faculty at your institution?

5. How do you define lifelong learning? How do you prepare students to realize that definition of lifelong learning through your teaching, department and college curriculum, and the undergraduate experience?

6. Much is made these days of student or classroom incivility, but what is inappropriate behavior for faculty in meetings and discussions? What are some possible solutions?

7. What sort of initiatives and motivation are useful and appropriate for faculty? How would you advise someone in a dean or provost's position to approach the task of motivation? Introducing and gaining support for new initiatives?

Chapter 22

1. Sports and undergraduate education have been a common link for the great majority of colleges and universities at all levels. That link raises several questions. For example, what benefits do organized sports offer to students and faculty at your institution? What is the real educational value of such sports for the student body? For the athletes? What is the supporting evidence for positive answers to the foregoing questions? Are sports programs at your institution assessed like other areas of the curriculum for educational outcomes?

2. Do modern sports programs for men and women have any proven connection with the specific educational mission of your college and university? What exactly is the student athlete? Does your institution have a definition?

3. What would an ideal sports program look like at your institution that would blend with and enhance campus learning? What would be the guiding principles for such an athletic program?

Chapter 24

1. What elements and benchmarks would you list in attempting to define a successful career as a college professor?
2. What would be on a listing of your job responsibilities and the hours you spend each week fulfilling these responsibilities? What changes would you most like to see in that description to help fulfill your definition of success as a college professor?
3. What do you like best about teaching and working with students?
4. Leo asks, "How would you build the perfect professor?" What would be your response?
5. What does a teacher need to know about students to be successful in the classroom? What kind of a survey would you construct for the first week of class to find out more about your students? What other sources of information and strategies can you employ?

Chapter 26

1. How would you answer President DaVita's question: "If you could create an undergraduate liberal arts college or university to best fit students to meet the demands of the twenty-first century, what would that institution be?"